Michael LeFebvre offers a new perspective on the so-called 'Worship Wars'. His view is that praise as worship in our churches has suffered diminution not only with the emergence of the recent praise song craze, but with the rise of eighteenth century hymnody as well. His complaint about the latter is that the range of topics has been narrowed and with it the loss of fullness of emotional expression because certain topics such as divine wrath upon the disobedient, found in the imprecatory Psalms, is lacking (this is only one example). His plea is that our churches would gain spiritually if the psalter were reintroduced. Speaking to God in words that He has chosen, with the breadth and depth of topics He has revealed, instead of singing about Him, would enrich our worship. I find *Singing the Songs of Jesus* a book worth the read. Yes, it will prove a learning experience for our congregations, but the dimensional richness the Psalms afford would be well worth the effort. I highly commend this volume for your own personal spiritual reflection as well as for that of our corporate worship.

JOHN D. HANNAH,
Distinguished Professor of Historical Theology,
Research Professor of Theological Studies,
Dallas Theological Seminary, Dallas, Texas

It has been wisely said that the Psalter is a spiritual cardiograph. The Psalms accurately reflect our spiritual health. The more I am 'at home' in singing the Psalms, the spiritually fitter I am. Uniquely in the Bible, the Psalms both speak to us – Luther derived much of his theology from the Psalter, – and also speak for us. They are the God-given words with which we can address both our Heavenly Father and each other. Michael LeFebvre's book is both scholarly and readable, and provides a wonderful incentive to 'Sing the Psalms, again'.

JONATHAN FLETCHER,
Vicar, Emmanuel Church, Wimbledon, London

D1580627

In this volume Michael LeFebvre enriches the church with wisdom regarding the vital role that singing the Psalms has in the worship of the church and the life of the believer. Michael avoids the hard edged heated opinions which often cloud this subject and instead casts refreshing pastoral light on a much neglected topic. All readers of this volume will be edified, educated and blessed!"

ANTHONY SELVAGGIO,
Teaching Elder, Rochester Reformed Presbyterian Church,
Rochester, New York

Singing the Songs of Jesus powerfully reminds us that the church has for too long ignored a vibrant source of devotion – the song book of Jesus. Even if you do not believe that they are the only songs that should be sung in the church, as some Christians do, we can't afford to neglect this divinely inspired song book that God has given us.

DONALD W. SWEETING,
President, Professor of Church History,
Reformed Theological Seminary, Orlando, Florida

This book should admirably fulfil the author's purpose by forcing those who have rejected or neglected the psalms in their praise to think again. Its central theory (that the psalms consist of praise conversations between God, his Messiah and his people) should help to illuminate the status of the psalter as the New Covenant song book it was meant to be and sheds much needed light on such dark areas as the imprecatory (cursing) psalms. If you have never sung the psalms and would like good biblical rather than historical reasons for doing so, and, crucially, if you want the key to understanding what you sing, you should really read this book .

KENNETH STEWART,
Minister, Dowanvale Free Church of Scotland, Glasgow.

Singing the Songs of Jesus

Revisiting the Psalms

Michael LeFebvre

To Roy Blackwood,
who taught me much
about the kingship of Jesus
and introduced me
to the singing of his Psalms.

Copyright © Michael Lefebvre 2010

ISBN 978-1-84550-600-1

First published in 2010
by
Christian Focus Publications Ltd,
Geanies House, Fearn, Ross-shire
IV20 1TW, Scotland
www.christianfocus.com

A CIP catalogue record for this book is available
from the British Library.

Cover design by moose77.com

Printed by Bell & Bain, Glasgow

Mixed Sources
Product group from well-managed forests and other controlled sources
www.fsc.org   Cert no. TT-COC-002769
© 1996 Forest Stewardship Council

Contents

About the Author

Michael LeFebvre is the pastor at Christ Church of Brownsburg, Indiana. His interest in the subject of worship is both longstanding and personal. One of his earliest memories is singing in the children's choir one Christmas at the Congregational Church his family attended during his pre-school years. When he was about seven, his family began attending a Lutheran Church. There, he grew in faith and love for Christ in the context of the traditional Lutheran liturgy. During the charismatic renewal movement of the 1970s and 80s, the family church gradually replaced the Lutheran prayer book with contemporary choruses and the old pipe organ with electric guitars and praise bands. Growing up in the middle of a church transforming from liturgical worship to contemporary, charismatic worship had an impact on Michael's interest in the theology of worship. It fostered an early awareness that worship practices are important, but not all churches worship the same way. It also became the seedbed for his interest in what the Bible has to say about the kinds of songs a church should be singing.

In 1988, Michael moved to Chicago to work with the Institute in Basic Life Principles where he helped write curriculum materials used by that ministry, including close collaboration with hymnologist Dr. Al Smith on the research and writing of hymn histories. During that period he worshiped at a traditional Baptist Church known for its commitment to classical hymns and quality musical accompaniment, which left him with a deep and abiding appreciation for the songs of the 17th to 19th century hymn writing movement.

After seven years in parachurch ministry, Michael developed a desire to serve in the local church. In 1995, he left his job in Chicago and began work as a freelance writer while exploring opportunities to prepare for the pastorate. One of the ministers he talked to about studying for the ministry was Dr. Roy Blackwood, now pastor emeritus of Second Reformed Presbyterian Church in Indianapolis. While visiting that congregation, Michael was impressed by the commitment to discipleship and doctrine he saw there, and he moved to Indianapolis. For the next ten years, Michael pursued theological studies part time while continuing his freelance writing job. He started his studies at Second RPC in Indianapolis, completing an MDiv at Reformed Presbyterian Theological Seminary in Pittsburgh, and then pursuing a PhD in biblical studies from the University of Aberdeen. During those years, he also carried on exegetical and theological study of Psalm singing, the fruits of which are compiled into this book.

Michael's PhD research included study in the arrangement of the Psalms, with a particular focus on the role of Psalm 1 as an introduction to the Psalter. It was the delight in God's law taught by Psalm 1 that led him to his final dissertation project on the function of biblical law in ancient Israel. This was published in T&T Clark's LHBOTS series, as *Collections, Codes, and Torah: The Re-characterization of Israel's Written Law* (2006). Other books written by Michael include, *William Symington: Penman of the Scottish Covenanters* (co-authored with Roy Blackwood; 2009) and the forthcoming, *Our Triune God: Living in the Love of the Three-in-One* (co-authored with Phil Ryken; due in 2011). He is also a contributor to an edited volume on the history of Psalm singing, *Sing a New Song* (edited by Anthony Selvaggio and Joel Beeke; 2010).

Preface

A Psalm Singer's
Introduction to the Psalms

Growing up in the church, I learned from childhood that Israel sang the Psalms in Old Testament times. But it never occurred to me that the church, today, could still sing them. I did learn Psalm choruses in the church of my youth, choruses like 'This is the Day' (from Ps. 118:24) and 'He Has Made Me Glad' (from Ps. 100:4). Nonetheless, I grew up with the idea that Israel sang the Psalms a long time ago, but today we mainly read them.

Then, as a young man, I moved to a church that sang the Psalms – all 150 of them. It was not love at first sight. Singing the Psalms seemed awkward. All that moaning and groaning. So much talk of confusion and judgment, of sacrifices and temple festivals. Frankly, the Psalms seemed hard to understand. Of course, the Psalms are in the Bible so who can fault singing them? But I still believed that hymns like 'A Mighty Fortress' were better suited for the church's praise.

Today, I still enjoy the songs of Martin Luther, Charles Wesley, and other great hymnwriters. But I have grown to love singing the Psalms. I have come to realize that my early discomfort with Psalm singing was not because of something awkward about them – the problem was with me. I had never been taught what a Psalm is. I had never learned how a Psalm is to be used, or what I should expect while singing them. Only through continued experience singing the Psalms in church, through lessons I learned from other Psalm singers, and by studying the patterns of praise in the Scriptures, did I begin to discover the principles of Psalm singing which I am now offering to you in this book.

This book is addressed to those who are curious about *singing* the Psalms. This is not a book about how to study the Psalms, it is a book about how to use them in personal praise and in corporate worship. There are plenty of other books available for those who want help studying the Psalms. My purpose in this book is to explain how the Psalms work as Christian praise songs.

The Book of Psalms used to be the primary hymnal of the church. In past centuries, singing the Psalms was the norm in Christian worship and singing other hymns was the exception. Is that an oddity of old fashioned religion that we have wisely 'moved beyond,' or is there something we can learn today from that historic devotion to Psalm singing?

I believe we are missing something in the church today by just reading the Psalms, and not singing them. Christians today will be enriched by rediscovering the historic practice of singing the Psalms in worship. Songs and hymns like those of Isaac Watts, P. P. Bliss, and others make important contributions to the church's devotional life. But the difference between such songs and the Psalms of the Bible is not simply a difference in age or a matter of clarity (yes, the Psalms can be hard to understand sometimes). The Psalms are qualitatively different from all other songs of Christian devotion in at least two key ways explained in this book.

Suppose that Christopher Columbus had found a detailed map of the entire New World on his first landing in 1492. But thinking the intricately painted skin he had found was just a specimen of native artwork, he simply hung it on the wall of his cabin to admire. Meanwhile, we picture Columbus and his men sketching tiny coasts here and there as they explore, supposing their simple maps to be great discoveries. All the while, there hangs on the wall above them a beautiful map already prepared – but they never realize it.

The modern church's attitude to the Psalms is not unlike this fanciful tale of Columbus and his painted map. Christian artists compose songs that describe our experiences of Jesus and his work in our lives. Such songwriting is a wonderful exercise in Christian piety. But how tragic it is that we fail to appreciate the rich, divinely crafted hymn book given to us by God – a hymn book God has given his church to use, not simply to admire as the songs of others long ago.

In this book, I hope to help twenty-first century Christians rediscover the value of the Psalms for singing. Ultimately, learning to use the Psalms is like learning to ride a bike: the best way is to get up and do it. And to keep doing it, until you get the sense of this valuable form of hymnody. I have put some ideas on a separate page at the end of each chapter to help the reader take the principles discussed along the way, and put them into practice. It may be that some reading this book are already Psalm singers; I hope this book will help them to sing the Psalms even more thoughtfully and profitably.

For those readers aware of the 'exclusive Psalmody' position to which some churches hold, I want to say that this book is not an argument about *exclusive* Psalmody. I am part of a denomination that sings only the Psalms in worship (the Reformed Presbyterian Church), and I do share that conviction.

But I will leave to other books the question of whether only the Psalms should be sung in worship. Instead, my desire is to see hymn and chorus singing Baptists, Lutherans, Presbyterians, Methodists, and all branches of the church include more Psalm singing in their worship. I am taking from the riches of churches with a long heritage of Psalm singing to give to those less acquainted with it.

May Jesus Christ, who sang the Psalms with his disciples so long ago, continue to make his presence known to us as we sing his Psalms in the church today!

Michael LeFebvre
Brownsburg, Indiana

1

The Psalms: Book or Hymnal –
and Does it Matter?

The German pastor and theologian, Dietrich Bonhoeffer, famously asked this question about the Psalms: How did these
words which men sang to God come to be regarded as words
from God to man? That is, if the Psalms were composed for
worshipers to lift their thoughts (by singing) up to God, why
do we now study them (by reading) as thoughts from God
down to us?[1]

God designed most books of the Bible to be read as his words
to us. When we read Genesis, we listen as God speaks to us
about the origins of the nations. When we read the Gospel of
John, we listen as God speaks to us about the life and teachings
of Jesus. This is how we should receive sixty-five of the Bible's
sixty-six books. But the Psalmbook is different: it alone is
composed as a collection of songs from men to God. They are
no less God's inspired word (more on that shortly), but of all
the Bible's books, in the Psalms we receive an exceptional gift
designed to become our words to God.

---

1   B. Childs, *Introduction to the Old Testament*, 513.

There are other books of songs in the Bible. Prophets, like Isaiah and Jeremiah, composed much of their writings in song-like poetry. But these 'lyrical prophecies' are songs from God to his people (cf., Zeph. 3:17). The Song of Solomon, also, is an entire book of songs, but it is not designed for people to sing to God. It is a collection of inspired love songs between idealized lovers. With the exception of the Psalms, the many song-filled books of the Bible are addressed to God's people: in them, God's truth sings to us.

The Book of Psalms is unique. It is a hymnal. It is the only book of the Bible with God as the audience and God's people as its appointed speakers. This is an important feature of the Psalms with significance for how we should use them in the church today.

The Psalms are words for God's people to sing to him. This does not mean the Psalms are any less God's Word to us than other books of the Bible. The fact is, the Spirit of God inspired these Psalms for us. They are, therefore, useful for instruction, reproof, correction, and training in righteousness with the rest of God-breathed Scripture (2 Tim. 3:16). The Psalms are worthy of study and useful for preaching as God's Word to us. But because they are inspired hymns, God has given us these words for a further purpose also. In the Psalms, God speaks to us about the things we need to sing to him.

We see both these uses of the Psalms – as God's words to men and man's words to God – modeled in the New Testament. In 1 Corinthians 15:25–7, the Apostle Paul wrote about Jesus, 'He must reign... for "God has put all things into subjection under his feet."' In that passage, Paul quotes Psalm 8:6 as God's word to us about Christ. Like the rest of Scripture, the Psalms are God's inspired word to us. But Acts 4:23–31 illustrates the further use unique to the Psalms.

In that passage, Peter and John led the Jerusalem congregation in singing the second Psalm to God: 'They lifted up their voices together to God and said [or sang], "Why did the Gentiles rage, and the peoples plot in vain? The kings of the earth set themselves, and the rulers were gathered together, against the Lord and against his Anointed.'" The Jerusalem believers put their own sufferings under godless rulers into an ancient Psalm about 'conspiring kings,' and the words of Psalm 2 became their own words in song to God.

Like the rest of Scripture, the Psalms are fully God's Word to us. But unlike the rest of Scripture, the Psalms are further designed to become our words to sing back to God. And the New Testament church continued to sing them. Why then, as Bonhoeffer asked, does the modern church (at least the Protestant church) see the Psalms only as God's Word to us?

In the pages that follow, we are going to look for the answer to Bonhoeffer's question.[2] Let me explain why this is important. It is not particularly important to know when this shift occurred. Finding a date for the decline of Psalm singing may be an interesting detail of history. But that is not the reason this question is important. What we need to find out is why this change occurred. If we can discover why the church stopped singing Psalms, we will better understand the issues that we need to address to recover fruitful Psalm singing.

Let's start our search for the answer to this question with the use of the Psalms in the Old and New Testament periods.

The Psalms in the Old and New Testaments

During the First Temple period, the singing of Psalms accompanied the public reading of Scripture. According to

2   The survey will, of course, be cursory. It also will focus on the history leading up to the Reformation/Protestant church experience. For documentation and a more thorough review of Psalm singing in church history, including more references for Roman Catholic and Eastern Orthodox traditions:: M. Patrick, *Story of the Church's Song*; J. Alexander Lamb, *Psalms in Worship*; W. Holladay, *Psalms through 3000 Years*.

Deuteronomy 31:11, Moses wrote the books of the Law for proclamation in worship and 1 Chronicles 15–16 reports that David wrote Psalms for singing in worship.[3] Second Chronicles describes a temple worship service, saying, 'The whole assembly worshiped, and the singers sang…And the officials commanded the Levites to sing praises to the LORD with the words of David and of Asaph the seer…' (2 Chron. 29:28–30).

After the Babylonian captivity, the Second Temple was built. Public reading and preaching was reinstituted (e.g., Neh. 8). Congregational singing of the Psalms was also restored: 'And they sang responsively, praising and giving thanks to the LORD [singing], "For he is good, for his stedfast love endures forever toward Israel" (Ezra 3:11, singing Ps. 136).

The singing of the Psalms continued through the tumultuous, intertestamental years, when the Greeks and later the Romans conquered Palestine. Among the records of the Maccabean wars (167–160 BC), for instance, we find this description of a praise assembly after a victorious battle: 'On their return they sang hymns and praises to Heaven – "For he is good, for his mercy endures forever" (1 Mac. 4:24 NRSV, singing Ps. 136). The Psalms continued to be sung through the intertestamental times, into the New Testament period.

When Jesus came, he preached from the Old Testament writings (e.g., Luke 24:44). He also sang the Psalms to the Father. For instance, in Mark 14:26, Jesus led his disciples in singing the Passover Psalms (Pss. 113–118).[4] On the cross, Jesus used one of the Psalms of lament to lift his cry of sorrow to heaven: 'And about the ninth hour Jesus cried out with a loud

3   For more on Israel's hymnody prior to David's Psalms, see: M. LeFebvre, 'The Hymns of Christ: The Old Testament Formation of the New Testament Hymnal.'

4   D. Kidner, *Psalms 73–150*, p401; L. Allen, *WBC: Psalms 101–150*, 134; J. Jeremias, *Eucharistic Words*, 255–61.

voice, saying, "My God, my God, why have you forsaken me?'"
(Matt. 27:46, citing Ps. 22:1). The author of Hebrews also tells
us that Jesus sang the Psalms (Heb. 2:11–12; 10:5).

After Christ's ascension, the New Testament church continued singing the Psalms. We have already noted the hymn
service reported in Acts 4. Likewise, Paul instructed the New
Testament churches to lift their praises which was to involve
'singing psalms' (Col. 3:16; cf., Eph. 5:26; see also 1 Cor. 14:26;
James 5:13).

Throughout Old Testament, intertestamental, and into
New Testament times, the Psalms were consistently sung. The
Psalms were read and preached (e.g., Acts 2:14–36; Heb. 1), but
they were also the church's song book through the biblical
periods. Bonhoeffer's shift, where the Psalms came to be used
primarily for reading, had not occurred in biblical times.

The Psalms in the Early Church

The example of Psalm singing by the New Testament apostles
laid the foundation for centuries after them. Hymn historian
Millar Patrick explains, 'The Psalter naturally became the
hymn-book of the Church from the beginning. The early
Christian writings bear constant witness to the use made of
it in private and public worship. In due time [new] Christian
hymnody arose, but the psalms never lost their place of
primacy.'[5]

John Chrysostom was one of the great preachers of the Early
Church, ministering in Constantinople in the 4th century.
Chrysostom reflects the love of Psalm singing in his day, 'If we
keep vigil [at night] in the church, David comes first, last, and
midst. If early in the morning…first, last, and midst is David
again…O marvellous wonder! Many who have made but little

5   M. Patrick, *Story of the Church's Song,* 14.

progress in literature, many who have scarcely mastered its first principles, have the Psalter by heart.[6]

New hymns were eventually written, as well.[7] For example, an unnamed poet composed this early hymn based on the angels' song in Luke 2:14:

> *Glory to God in the highest,*
> *and on earth peace, good will among men.*
> *We praise Thee, we bless Thee,*
> *we worship Thee, we glorify Thee,*
> *we give thanks to Thee for Thy great glory...*
> *For Thou only art holy; Thou only art the Lord,*
> *O Jesus Christ, to the glory of God the Father. Amen.*[8]

Even when new songs appeared, however, they never supplanted the singing of Psalms. They supplemented Psalm singing. Throughout the Early Church years, the Psalms continued to be sung in Christian worship.

---

6   J. Neale and R. Littledale, *Psalms*, 1.1–2.

7   The observation that hymnwriting took place in the Early Church may be troubling to readers who hold to exclusive psalmody. Other readers may cite this as evidence against the exclusive psalmody position. In my desire to avoid delving into that debate in this book, let me simply note for the sake of all readers that there were new songs written during the early centuries, but even then it was controversial. In the Early Church, as today, there were some who held that only the Psalms should be sung in worship, while others believed new hymns could also be used in worship. One 4th century church council, for instance, sought to clarify the matter, ruling, 'No psalm composed by private individuals nor any uncanonical books may be read in the church...' (Canon LIX from the Council of Laodicea.) In other words, the presence of hymnwriting in the Early Church does not prove either side right; it simply illustrates that the controversy has a long history.

8   Translation from the English website of the Russian Orthodox Church: http://en.liturgy.ru/nav/utrena/utren15.php (accessed on Nov 10, 2008).

The Psalms in Medieval Worship

Protestants often have a dim view of the medieval years. This is unfortunate. God was doing great things among his people in those centuries between the fall of Rome and the Reformation. Nevertheless, there were also religious developments in those centuries which the Reformers would later reject as unbiblical.

Pope Gregory the Great (540–604) introduced the so-called 'Gregorian chants' into church worship during this period. This enchanting musical style was intended to increase the otherworldliness of cathedral services, intensifying the sense of heavenliness in worship. In fact, to further ensure the 'heavenliness' of the church's praise, professional choirs began to take over the singing. Even if well intentioned, this was a tragic shift in worship. Singing was taken away from the congregation altogether. But the Psalms were still sung.

The Psalms continued to be the primary source of church praise. Both the Eastern Orthodox and Roman Catholic service calendars (the Daily Offices) called for the cathedral choirs to sing through the entire Psalmbook, beginning to end, every week.

The Psalms were also sung in private homes. Although the laity was not singing in worship services, they sang Psalms in their own daily routines. Among the wealthy who could afford it, many purchased their own copies of the Psalms for private, devotional singing. King Alfred the Great (849–899) spent time singing Psalms every day and carried the Psalms with him for that purpose.[9]

It is ironic, but even in that period when congregational singing ceased, Christians continued singing Psalms.

---

9   W. Holladay, *Psalms through 3000 Years*, 177–8.

The Psalms in the Reformation

The recovery of congregational singing was one of the great hallmarks of the Reformation. Martin Luther exclaimed, 'The substance of worship is, that our dear Lord speaks with us through his holy word, and we in return speak with him through prayer and song of praise.'[10]

Luther was a skilled musician, himself. He taught the people to sing the biblical Psalms again, and he composed new hymns which he called, 'German psalms for the people.' One of his most famous hymns is 'A Mighty Fortress' – a favorite of many to this day.

Other Reformers, like John Calvin, shared the same passion for congregational singing. Calvin did not share Luther's practice of writing new hymns, but he also promoted congregational Psalmody, commissioning the translation of the Psalms into metrical verse for the churches of Geneva. The completed *Genevan Psalter* was published in 1562. Calvin also set up Psalm singing classes in the Geneva schools. That way, when churches met for worship, the children knew how to sing the Psalms and could help the adults learn them, too. Reformation churches in other lands also produced metrical Psalters. Thomas Sternhold and Thomas Hopkin's *Whole Booke of Psalmes* (1562) became the songbook of Reformation churches in England, and the *Scottish Psalter* (1564) in the Presbyterian churches of Scotland.

One visitor to Calvin's Geneva described his experience with congregational Psalm singing in this way: '[When the congregation is assembled,] each one draws from his pocket a small book which contains the psalms with notes, and out of full hearts, in the native speech, the congregation sings before

10   M. Patrick, *Story of the Church's Song,* 72.

and after the sermon. Every one testifies to me how great the consolation and edification is derived from this custom.'[11]

The Psalms were still regarded as hymns designed for God's people to sing to him. John Calvin recognized this unique character of the Psalms, as the one book in the Bible designed to be used as men's words to God:

> The other parts of Scripture contain the commandments which God enjoined his servants to announce to us. But here [in the Psalms] the prophets themselves, seeing they are exhibited to us as speaking to God, and laying open all their inmost thoughts and affections, call, or rather draw, each of us to [participate]...[12]

The shift in attitude toward the Psalter – regarding it primarily as a book from God rather than hymns to God – had not yet occurred. To answer Bonhoeffer's question of how the Psalms came to be regarded as a book and not a hymnal, we need to look into the centuries after the Reformers.

The Psalms in Post-Reformation Protestantism

God's people sang the Psalms from at least the 10th century before Christ (the time of King David) until the 16th and 17th centuries after Christ (the time of the Reformation). Other hymns written during these millenia supplemented the Psalms, but never replaced them. It was only in the 18th century A.D., with the modern hymnwriting movement, that an effort to replace Psalm singing emerged.

One of the most important contributors to this movement was Isaac Watts (1674–1748), commonly called 'The Father of English Hymnody.' Watts did not start the movement, but

11   M. Patrick, *Story of the Church's Song,* 92.
12   Calvin, *Psalms,* xxxvii.

he was one of its most prolific poets (he composed around 650 hymns). He was also a prominent spokesman for the movement.

In the preface to one of his hymnals, Watts explained the problem with Psalm singing in his day:

> To see the dull indifference, the negligent and thoughtless air, that sits upon the faces of the whole assembly while the psalm is on their lips, might tempt even a charitable observer to suspect [i.e., to question] the fervour of inward religion...That very action which should elevate us to the most delightful and divine sensations, doth not only flatten our devotion, but too often awakes our regret, and touches all the springs of uneasiness within us.'[13]

This is certainly a tragic description of Christian praise. The English hymnwriters wanted to help Christians re-engage their hearts in their praise. We cannot fault this desire. But was their method really called for – to replace the Psalms with new hymns?

When Watts said that Psalm singing 'too often awakes our regret' and 'touches all the springs of uneasiness within us,' he was refering to the prominent expressions of judgment and lament throughout the Psalms. These, in the view of the new hymnwriters, were 'sub-Christian' sentiments unfitting for Christian worship. 'There are elements in the Psalms distinctly Jewish,' W. Garrett Horder wrote in 1889, 'and expressive of the feeling of earlier days. There are imprecatory notes that are out of harmony with the gentler melody of Christ. These ought to be dropped as unsuitable to *Christian* worship....'[14]

Religious historian Stephen Marini further explains:

---

13   I. Watts, *Psalms of David Imitated,* xxvii–viii.

14   W. Horder, *Hymn Lover,* 24–25. (Italics original.)

[Watts] insisted…that the Psalms themselves required modification for Christian worship. While he granted that David was unquestionably a chosen instrument of God, Watts claimed that his religious understanding could not have fully apprehended the truths later revealed through Jesus Christ. The Psalms should therefore be 'renovated' as if David had been a Christian, or as Watts put it in the title of his 1719 metrical psalter, they should be 'imitated in the language of the New Testament.'[15]

The full title of Watts's 1719 hymnal was, *The Psalms of David Imitated in the Language of the New Testament and Applied to the Christian State and Worship*. To 'imitate' a Psalm, Watts distilled topics of praise from it, left behind 'uneasy' features (like complaints and imprecation), and then rewrote those topics of praise in new poetry applied to the British empire ('the Christian State')[16] and the church ('Christian Worship').

Let me offer an example. The first book published on the American continent was the *Bay Psalm Book* of 1640. This was a generation before the new hymnwriters, and the *Bay Psalm Book* was a faithful translation of the Psalms for singing. In it, Psalm 137 ended with these graphic lines of imprecation:

15 S. Marini, *Sacred Song in America,* p76. Watts wrote an essay explaining his views on renovating the Psalms and adding new hymns as an appendix to his 1707 hymnal, *Hymns and Spiritual Songs*. That essay was called, 'A Short Essay Toward the Improvement of Psalmody: Or, An Enquiry how the Psalms of David ought to be translated into Christian Songs, and how lawful and necessary it is to compose other Hymns according to the clearer Revelations of the Gospel, for the Use of the Christian Church.'

16 In his zeal to make the themes of the Psalms relevant for his British compatriots, some accuse Watts of going too far in identifying the throne of Messiah with the throne of Britain in his hymns, thereby laying the groundwork for the emerging theology of British imperialism. (E.g., J. Hull, 'From Educator to Theologian,' 91–106.)

> *Blest shall he be, that payeth thee,*
> *Daughter of Babylon,*
> *Who must be waste: that which thou hast*
> *Rewarded us upon.*
> *O happy he shall surely be*
> *That taketh up, that eke*
> *Thy little ones against the stones*
> *Doth into pieces break.*

There is no denying it, these are troubling words! Words of judgment are supposed to be sobering. But under the spirit of the new hymnody, these words were also deemed unfit for use in Christian praise. A century and a half after the *Bay Psalm Book,* a new collection of Psalms 'imitated' was published in Massachusetts. Here is the song based on Psalm 137 in that 1801 edition of *The Psalms of David*:

> *Jesus, thou Friend divine,*
> *Our Savior and our King,*
> *Thy hand from every snare and foe*
> *Shall great deliverance bring.*
> *Sure as thy truth shall last*
> *To Zion shall be given*
> *The highest glories earth can yield,*
> *And brighter bliss of heaven.*[17]

The theme of devotion to Mount Zion had been taken from Psalm 137, and a new hymn composed around it. Far from translations of the Psalms, these 'imitations' were essentially new hymns. Other new hymns (not intended as Psalm updates) were also widespread in the 18th and 19th centuries,

---

17   This particular comparison was brought to my attention by: Leaver, 'The Hymn Explosion,' 14. The hymnal quotations are taken from that article.

blossoming under 19th century American hymnwriters like
Fanny Crosby, P. P. Bliss, and Ira Sankey. By the late 19th century Psalm singing had been eclipsed, and by the mid-20th
century it was virtually unheard of.

We do not need to discredit the intentions of the modern-
era hymnwriters, nor demean the value of the religious poetry
they produced. But we do need to ask whether it was right for
churches to adopt this new wave of songs as *replacements* for
Psalm singing. Are aspects of the Psalms 'unsuitable to Christian worship'? Is the religious understanding of the Psalms
insufficient for New Testament, Christ-centered praise? Watts
and his peers answered 'yes' to these questions for the first
time in church history, overturning millenia of the Psalter's
primacy as the praise book of God's people. With this movement, we have found the answer to Bonhoeffer's question. The
church stopped using the Psalms as human words to God.
Watts and the other hymnwriters certainly introduced a bold
'reform' of Christian worship. Were they right? The 'problems'
of the Psalms that led to their movement are the issues we will
need to examine in the following chapters of this book.

For now, let me note the striking contrast between Watts's
perception of Psalm singing and that of Calvin's Geneva a
few generations earlier. In Watts's description quoted earlier,
Psalm singing 'awakes regret…and uneasiness' in the congregation. But the Genevan churches of Calvin's day found 'great
consolation and edification' in Psalm singing, as earlier noted.
This contrast suggests that there was a different expectation of
praise songs between the two periods – an expectation which
the Psalms beautifully satisfied in Calvin's Geneva and a different expectation which the Psalms actually offended in Watts's
England.

Of the nineteen Psalms included in the first Psalter published
in Calvin's Geneva (in 1539), six were Psalms of repentance
(Pss. 25, 32, 36, 51, 103, 130), six were Psalms about judgment

and subduing enemies (Pss. 2, 3, 46, 91, 114, 137, 143), three were Psalms about the law and righteousness (Pss. 1, 15, 19), and only three were Psalms of praise (Pss. 104, 113, 138).[18] Many Christians today would be shocked to learn that the imprecatory Psalm 137 was part of the first Reformation hymnal in Geneva. A different standard of praise in Watts's day dismissed the kinds of Psalms which were found desirable in Calvin's day. As a result, the Psalms were put aside.

At least they were set aside as songs. The Psalms have remained a favorite text for devotional reading. There was no effort to delete the Psalms from the Bible; they were retained as words we read from God. But they were no longer sung back to God. The change pondered by Deitrich Bonhoeffer became widespread in the 19th and 20th centuries.[19]

We have lost something important when we treat the Psalms as a book rather than a hymnal. And the problem is bigger than simply singing the Psalms again. We have to rediscover the right standard of praise that our churches are supposed to expect of our songs. We must relearn why the Psalms are composed with so much agonizing and 'awkward' language in them. We have to rediscover how the Apostles, the Early Church Fathers, and the Reformers saw Christ in the Psalms in such glory that they esteemed them as the ideal praise book of Christ-centered worship. We have to find out what hymn singing is supposed to do, and how the Psalms supremely fulfill a need in the church which is going unmet when we fail to sing them.

Praise God for the beautiful songs written by gifted hymnwriters through the centuries. I still regard Watts's masterpiece,

18   J. Witvliet, 'Spirituality of the Psalter,' 278.

19   It should be noted: Bonhoeffer posed the question, not because he was in favor of treating the Psalter as primarily a book to read. As a Christian who suffered much in World War II Germany, Bonhoeffer personally used the Psalms as prayers and songs to God. For an excellent article on Bonhoeffer's own use of the Psalms, see: P. Miller, 'Bonhoeffer and the Psalms.'

'When I Survey the Wondrous Cross,' as a personal favorite. Christians can benefit greatly from these songs. But when extra-biblical songs are the diet of worship, and when they re-train our expectations so that the hymns God gave his church now seem 'unfit,' some kind of recovery operation is needed.

In the remaining chapters of this book, I hope to outline some biblical directions for that recovery. I want to look at what the Psalms do for us that no other hymns can do, and to give practical suggestions for Christians and churches to sing them again.

The best way to get acquainted with Psalm singing is to get a Psalter and start singing from it. The Psalms can be sung in congregational worship, and they are well suited for family devotions or personal quiet times as well. There are a number of songbooks to choose from for Psalm singing.

The Book of Psalms for Worship (Crown and Covenant, 2009) and *The Trinity Psalter* (Presbyterian Church in America, 1994) are two excellent Psalters used widely in Psalm singing churches across North America. The latter is also available in Braille. (These and other Psalm resources, including CD recordings, are available at www.crownandcovenant.com)

In the United Kingdom, these Psalters are available in addition to *Sing Psalms* (Free Church of Scotland, 2003), *The Psalms for Singing* (Cameron Press, 2004), and others. A beautiful, 12-volume CD set of Anglican choral Psalmody, *Psalms from St. Paul's,* is available on the Hyperion label.

For those interested in historical Psalm tunes, consider the *Book of Praise: Anglo-Genevan Psalter* (Canadian Reformed Churches, 2010). This Psalter provides modern English translations of all 150 Psalms, but uses the tunes from the sixteenth-century Psalter of John Calvin's Geneva. (It is available online at www.bookofpraise.ca) A selection of Spanish Psalms for singing is included in *El Himnario* (Church Publishing, 1998; selections 405–441 are Psalms).

Although Psalm singing is not common in the contemporary church, there are still plenty of Psalm singing resources available. For pastors and worship leaders interested in a more full list of Psalm-singing resources, let me recommend John D. Witvliet's *The Biblical Psalms in Christian Worship: A Brief Introduction and Guide to Resources* (Eerdmans, 2007).

2

The Power of Psalmody:
Two Specialties of the Biblical Psalms

'A rose is a rose is a rose,' or so they say. But are all roses the same? There are actually over a hundred different species of roses, and they are certainly not all alike.

What about worship songs? Is it fitting to suppose that 'a hymn is a hymn is a hymn'? There are modern songs, like Robin Mark's 'Days of Elijah.' There are choruses, like 'Our God is an Awesome God' (by Rich Mullins). There are classic hymns, like Henry F. Lyte's 'Abide with Me.' There are also early church songs from centuries ago, like the *Gloria Patria*:

> *Glory be to the Father, and to the Son,*
> *and to the Holy Ghost;*
> *As it was in the beginning, is now, and ever shall be,*
> *World without end. Amen, Amen.*

And there are the hymns of ancient Israel canonized in the Book of Psalms, like King David's 'LORD our Lord, How Majestic Your Name' (Ps. 8). In the church today, we possess a vast collection of songs extolling our redeeming God.

We often throw these songs together in our services with the assumption that they all accomplish the same purpose – as though 'a hymn is a hymn is a hymn.' We recognize there is a different 'feel' to a chorus versus an old hymn; but we generally treat these various categories of praises as accomplishing the same purpose: expressing our love for God.

In this chapter, I want to challenge that assumption. There is a profound difference between what the Psalms accomplish in worship and what all those other kinds of devotional songs can accomplish. We are not comparing apples and apples here. There are at least two characteristics of the Psalms that make them unique – and uniquely powerful – for modern Christian worship.

In order to demonstrate these two, distinctive features of the Psalms, I'd like to take you back to the hymnwriting workshops where some of the earliest Psalms were being composed. Imagine that we are back in ancient Israel, 3,500 years ago, during the reign of King David. He is just starting to compile new Psalms for use in the new temple he is designing.

David personally composed many of the hymns used in Israel's worship, but he also enlisted a team of assistants to work with him in this songwriting. It is in 1 Chronicles 25 where we read about the hymnwriting workshops King David organized to help him in this production. And in describing these hymn production centers to us, the Scriptures identify two features that distinguish the hymns of David's collection (the Psalms) from the hymns produced today.

Let me quote the first seven verses of that chapter, below. It is the kind of text that a reader is apt to skim through. On first blush, it just sounds like a lot of mundane detail. But as 'the devil is in the details' when things go wrong, 'God is in the details' when things are put together correctly. So let me encourage you to read these details of the hymnwriting workshops as God ordered them.

1 Chronicles 25:1–7

¹ David and the chiefs of the service also set apart for the service the sons of Asaph, and of Heman, and of Jeduthun, who prophesied with lyres, with harps, and with cymbals. The list of those who did the work and of their duties was:

² Of the sons of Asaph: Zaccur, Joseph, Nethaniah, and Asharelah, sons of Asaph, under the direction of Asaph, who prophesied under the direction of the king.

³ Of Jeduthun, the sons of Jeduthun: Gedaliah, Zeri, Jeshaiah, Shimei, Hashabiah, and Mattithiah, six, under the direction of their father Jeduthun, who prophesied with the lyre in thanksgiving and praise to the LORD.

⁴ Of Heman, the sons of Heman: Bukkiah, Mattaniah, Uzziel, Shebuel and Jerimoth, Hananiah, Hanani, Eliathah, Giddalti, and Romamti-ezer, Joshbekashah, Mallothi, Hothir, Ma-hazioth.

⁵ All these were the sons of Heman the king's seer, according to the promise of God to exalt him, for God had given Heman fourteen sons and three daughters.

⁶ They were all under the direction of their father in the music in the house of the LORD with cymbals, harps, and lyres for the service of the house of God. Asaph, Jeduthun, and Heman were under the order of the king.

⁷ The number of them along with their brothers, who were trained in singing to the LORD, all who were skillful, was 288.

David had received a covenant promise from God that his heirs would serve as the patrons of God's worship, forever (1 Chron. 17). After receiving that exalted responsibility, David began preparations for the temple and its operations. (By the way, 1 Chronicles 28:19 assures us that all David's preparations were made with divine direction.)

In chapter 22, David made material provisions for the temple: stockpiles of gold, bronze, silver, stone, and wood. In chapter 23, David set up the officers of the temple: he arranged the Levitical families into teams of judges, gatekeepers, musicians, and so forth. In chapters 24 to 26, we encounter specializations within those Levitical assignments – including the hymnwriting schools in chapter 25, quoted in part above.

The structure of these temple hymnwriting teams can be visualized as shown on the opposite page. David appointed three hymnwriters in his initial system: Asaph, Jeduthun, and Heman. Each of these, in turn, had sons working with him: four sons with Asaph; six with Jeduthun; and an impressive fourteen with Heman. Each of these sons was an expert instrumentalist and had a mini-ensemble of eleven other instrumentalists working with him (vv. 9–31 describe these ensembles of 12).

The result is an elaborate production center with twenty-four instrumental ensembles composing music for the hymns being written by the top three chiefs: Asaph, Jeduthun, and Heman. Elsewhere we learn that there was a 4,000 strong army of additional musicians to draw from for the temple services (1 Chron. 23:5). But it is this team, described in 1 Chronicles 25, which David set up to help produce Israel's worship hymns – the Psalms.

All this seems like a lot of detail. In fact, one commentator concludes, 'We find little of relevance in this material, [but] it was obviously of significance in the arrangement of worship in the [ancient] congregation.'[20] But there *is* tremendous relevance for us in this catalog of hymnic officers. As mundane as these matters may appear, God is teaching us lessons about worship in these details.

In every corner of the temple's arrangements, in every aspect of its rituals and every position within its structures, God was teaching his people important lessons on the forgiveness

20   R. Braun, *1 Chronicles,* p247.

Temple Hymnwriting Teams (1 Chr 25)

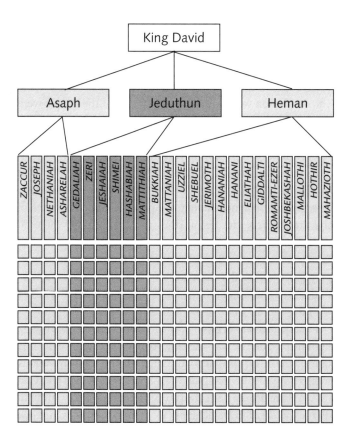

King David oversees three psalm-writing prophets, who in turn oversee 288 musicians in 24 teams of 12.

Christ was to accomplish, and the worship which the forgiven bring to God through Christ. The temple is a tangible lesson on the Gospel, as the writer of the New Testament book of Hebrews goes to great lengths to show us.

Two powerful features of hymnody are being taught in this Psalm production system of the Old Testament temple.

Hymns that are inspired

The first lesson we learn is that the hymns of the temple were *divinely inspired.* In 1 Chronicles 25:1–7, we are told no fewer than four times that prophetic inspiration was a prerequisite for writing worship songs in David's workshops.

In verse 1, we read that Asaph, Heman, and Jeduthun (the three chiefs) '*prophesied* with lyres, harps, and cymbals.' After this general statement about the prophetic qualifications of the three chiefs, the text further asserts the same for each of these three hymnwriters, individually. In verse 2, as the family of Asaph is enumerated, we are reminded that Asaph '*prophesied* under the direction of the king.' We are likewise told, at the end of Jeduthun's family list, 'Jeduthun *prophesied* with the lyre' (v. 3).

Finally, Heman is given special notice. He was not just a hymnic prophet; he was 'the king's seer' (v. 5). He was evidently one of the royal prophets consulted by the king in various matters of state. Like Nathan (e.g., 2 Sam. 7:2–4; 12:1) and Gad (e.g., 1 Sam. 22:5; 2 Sam. 24:11–13), Heman probably brought divine messages to David about all manner of things, not just hymns. As one of God's special promises to Heman (perhaps as a reward for his service in that capacity), Heman was granted many sons and given the added privilege of composing temple hymns. It would seem that song writing was a privileged role for a prophet. In any case, Heman (like Asaph and Jeduthun) wrote songs for Israel's worship under divine inspiration.

First Chronicles is careful – with fourfold repetition – to qualify Israel's hymnwriters as divinely inspired. Other passages in Scripture confirm this pattern, that Old Testament worship songs were divinely inspired (e.g., Exod. 15:1; Deut. 31:19; Ps. 40:3; 2 Sam. 23:1–2). This is one feature that sets apart the Psalms from all other songs composed in the church.

Some modern hymnwriters may be better poets than their counterparts in ancient Israel. Some of the songs produced in recent centuries may be easier to understand and more aesthetically pleasing to sing than the biblical Psalms. But the church has historically esteemed and treasured the Psalms because they alone are inspired and inerrant hymns. The fourth century church father, Athanasius of Alexandria (c. 293–373), wrote, 'Do not let anyone amplify these words of the Psalter with persuasive phrases of the profane [i.e., the uninspired], and do not let him attempt to recast or completely change the words…Their expressions [are] superior to those we construct…[for it is] the Spirit who speaks in the saints… [to] render assistance to us.'[21]

A century later, Augustine of Hippo (353–430) acknowledged the attractiveness of new songs, but he urged his fellow worshipers not to neglect the superiority of singing inspired Psalms. He wrote how some 'reproach us [for] our grave chanting of the divine songs of the prophets [i.e., the Psalms] in our churches, while they inflame their passions in their revels by the singing of psalms of human composition, which rouse them like the stirring notes of the trumpet of the battlefield.'[22] It was the integrity of the Psalms as God-breathed hymns, not their musical delight, which led Augustine to value them.

If we want only 'clear', 'gentle' songs in church, then we certainly can do a lot better than the angst, verbosity, ritual

---

21   Athanasius, 'Letter to Marcellinus,' 102–8.

22   Augustine, 'Letter to Januarius,' p1.315.

language, and oft obscure word pictures of the old Psalms. But if we are looking for hymns that instruct our faith and ground our souls in truth, there are no hymns more exciting and desirable than the inspired Psalms.

We cherish the stammering words of Moses (Exod 4:10), not because the Mosaic writings are easy to read but because they are divinely inspired. We give higher authority to the untrained speech of Amos (Amos 7:14) than the polished speeches of Aristotle, not because Amos is rhetorically superior to Aristotle, but because he was inspired by God. We treasure the run-on sentences and convoluted arguments of Paul, not because he is easy to read – even Peter admits Paul is hard to understand (2 Pet. 3:16) – but because Paul writes with divine inspiration.

In the same way, the church rightly cherishes the hymns given to us in the Psalmbook, not because they are easy or even the most eloquent of songs, but because they were carefully produced under divine inspiration. They are inerrant – without error. The Psalms are true in every point, and they are perfectly prepared for use by the Holy Spirit.

Many aspects of the Psalms *are* aesthetically rich and poetically compelling. There is great elegance and beauty in the Psalms. But even if we find modern songs to be more attractive, only the Psalms are flawless. Here is one capacity that the Davidic praise guilds had, which we cannot duplicate: divine inspiration. Divine inspiration is the first of the two, great distinctives that set apart the Psalms as a unique kind of hymn for the church.

What a gift for the church! God not only gives us inspired teaching in the Bible, but inspired songs too. Songs often do as much as sermons (if not more) to shape our faith. The Scriptures preached *and* the Psalms sung provide an ideal curriculum for shaping the faith of the church.

There are Psalms that teach the doctrine of sin (e.g., Pss 6; 25; 51), Psalms that teach about the final hope, or eschatology (e.g., Pss 1; 73; 149), and Psalms that unpack that ever perplexing relationship between divine sovereignty and human responsibility (e.g., Ps. 139). There are Psalms that teach us how to think about the church (e.g., Pss 48; 87), or about world missions (e.g., Pss 47; 96), or that shape our faith in the person and work of Christ (e.g., Pss 2; 22; 72; 89; 110). There are Psalms to guide us in every other department of holy doctrine. Martin Luther called the Book of Psalms a 'little Bible' because it provides a thorough summary of all biblical doctrine within the scope of its 150 songs.[23]

Many songs teach doctrine, but shouldn't we give primacy to the songs of that greatest of all theologians, the Holy Spirit? Comparing the catechetical value of the Psalms with the other doctrinal statements produced by the church, Scottish theologian James Denny urged, 'The Church's Confession of faith should be sung, not signed.'[24]

When a worshiper sings uninspired songs, he has to scrutinize the doctrine he is singing. Before I discovered Psalm singing, there were times in worship when I found myself wondering whether a song I was singing in worship was true. For instance, consider the classic Easter hymn by A. H. Ackley, 'He Lives.'

Alfred Ackley was shaving before church on Easter morning in 1932 with the radio on, when a radio minister said it really doesn't matter whether Jesus literally rose from the dead or not. The message of the resurrection, not the facts, the radio preacher rambled on, is what is important. Ackley was justly outraged, and spent that Easter Sunday pondering ways he

---

23   In the preface to his 1534 *Psalter,* Luther wrote, '[The Psalter] promises Christ's death and resurrection so clearly – and pictures of his kingdom and the condition and nature of all Christendom – that it might well be called a little Bible.' (M. Luther, *Luther's Works,* 35.254).

24   Cited in Anderson, 'Israel's Creed,' 277.

might prove to that radio minister that Jesus truly did rise from the dead. That night, he sat at his table and penned this hymn as his answer:

> *I serve a risen Savior,*
> *He's in the world today;*
> *I know that He is living,*
> *whatever men may say;*
> *I see his hand of mercy,*
> *I hear his voice of cheer,*
> *And just the time I need him,*
> *He's always near.*

> *He lives, he lives, Christ Jesus lives today!*
> *He walks with me and talks with me*
> *along life's narrow way.*
> *He lives, he lives, salvation to impart!*
> *You ask me how I know he lives:*
> *He lives within my heart.*

Jesus rose bodily from the grave, and the eyewitness testimony of the apostles is the evidence Scripture gives us for this assurance. What about Ackley's further proofs of the resurrection in his hymn? Is our confidence in the resurrection supported by our subjective experience of his presence in our lives? What about those times when we do not feel his presence?

I'm not trying to nitpick in raising this question, but to illustrate the kind of dilemma we face – even in the middle of a worship service – when our hymns are composed by men. Some churches will conclude that Ackley's hymn is theologically unsound and will not sing it. Others will conclude it is a doctrinally sound hymn, and sing it often. One church becomes further entrenched in a doctrine of the resurrection assured by personal experience; another branch of the church, otherwise. And thoughtful singers in both circles of churches will occasionally wonder as they sing, 'Is what I am singing really biblical?'

The beautiful thing about the Psalms is that they are above suspicion. Even if we wonder what a Psalm means, we never need to wonder if it is true. We can pour our hearts into them as we sing, without having to fear whether we are professing error.

Praise is more than an expression of our love for God. Singing is also part of the church's catechism. In a sense, congregational singing is that part of the service when the whole church takes part in preaching to one another (Col. 3:16). If the church today is to experience modern reformation, a return to sound preaching ought to be joined with a recovery of Psalm singing.

We will explore how the Psalms shape our faith, in greater detail, in chapter five of this book. But the first feature that supremely qualifies the Psalms for use in Christian praise is its *inspired* character.

King David went to great pains to set up hymn workshops in the temple that produced inspired hymns for God-fearing worship. The resulting praises were sung by God's people for centuries, and they have been preserved in the canon for us too.

Hymns that are king-led

There is a second prerequisite of hymnwriting in the guilds of King David. The songs prepared in the temple workshops were all *king-led*. Temple hymnwriters needed to have the king's imprimatur on each of the hymns they composed.

In 1 Chronicles 25:1, King David exercises his authority to appoint hymnwriters for God's worship: 'David and the chiefs of the service also set apart for the service the sons of Asaph, and of Heman, and of Jeduthun.' What is more significant, verse 2 tells us David continued to oversee the hymnwriters' work after their appointment.

Asaph, the first composing chief, 'prophesied *under the direction [lit., under the hand] of the king.*' A second time it is stated, in the summary of the hymn guilds in verse 6, that each of the three chiefs labored '*under the order [lit., under the hand] of the king.*' King David did not just set up these guilds and leave them to their work. He maintained ongoing, royal oversight of their hymn production.

David was 'the sweet psalmist of Israel' (2 Sam. 23:1); these men were his 'ghostwriters' so to speak, aiding him in what remained fundamentally his own responsibility. Others helped David and his heirs in the production of Psalms for worship, but the whole collection is rightly called 'the Psalms of David' because they all speak 'in the king's voice.'

We often assume that the role of the king in Israel was primarily political. The kings and queens we study in European history are generally thought of as political figures, but we make a mistake if we presume Israel's kings were just administrators and warriors. Kingship in the ancient world, including Israel, was a sacral office (e.g., Ps. 110:4).[25] In the Old Testament, Israel's king could be found at the head of worship processions, leading sacrifices at the altar on high holy days, interceding in prayer before God, and otherwise mediating the nation's worship – not just its politics or its wars. When Scripture identifies David as 'the sweet psalmist of Israel' (2 Sam. 23:1), this is not simply a statement affirming his musical talents. It is a statement of a royal office he held.

President Dwight D. Eisenhower enjoyed painting, but painting was not one of his duties in the White House. Leading the nation in singing was, however, a duty of the Davidic dynasty. As the patron of the temple and the representative of the people before God, the Davidic king was responsible to

---

25   The literature on this subject is extensive. Cf., A. Johnson, *Sacral Kingship in Israel*; J. Day, *King and Messiah*.

sing for Israel in worship, and the nation joined with him in his hymns.[26]

This is a second facet of what a Psalm facilitates in worship. *In biblical worship, it is the king who leads the congregation into worship, and it is the king's own songs that the congregation sings with him.* This principle is seen in the royal oversight of the hymn workshops of 1 Chronicles 25. It is also seen in the pattern of worship described throughout the Scriptures.

The book of Genesis does not tell us much about the worship practices of ancient patriarchs like Enoch, Noah, and Abraham. We are told about their sacrifices and their prayers. We might suspect that they sang too (hymns were part of many ancient religions in those times). If the patriarchs did sing in worship before the altar, Genesis does not record anything about their songs. It is at the point of the exodus from Egypt that Scripture begins to detail the worship practices of Israel.

Israel had gone down into Egypt as a *family* of 70 people, but they came out as a *nation* of 600,000 men (plus women and children). Organizing this new nation, God gave Moses instructions for their laws and for their worship. The first reported songleader for Israel was Moses himself. After crossing the Red Sea, with pharaoh's chariots drowned beneath the waves, Moses composed and led the first recorded congregational hymn in the Bible:

---

26   There is an old, rabbinic parable used for centuries to explain that title 'sweet psalmist of Israel.' According to the parable, 'There was a company of musicians that sought to sing a hymn to the king. The king said the them: To be sure, all of you are sweet singers, all of you are musicians, all of you have superior skill, all of you are men worthy of taking part in the singing of a hymn to the king, yet let the hymn, in whose singing all of you will take part, bear the name of only one man among you because his voice is the sweetest of all your voices. Thus it is written, *The saying of David the son of Jesse ... the sweet singer of the Psalms of Israel.*' (W. Braude, *Midrash on the Psalms*, 1.6.)

> *I will sing unto the Lord,*
> *for he has triumphed gloriously;*
> *the horse and rider he has thrown into the sea...*
> *(Exod. 15:1–21)*

Many years later, the people stood in Moab ready to cross into the Promised Land. There, Moses preached a series of sermons which form the book of Deuteronomy. After finishing his sermons and writing them into a book (Deut. 31:9, 24–6), he also taught Israel a new hymn: 'Then Moses spoke [or, sang] the words of this song…in the ears of all the assembly of Israel:'

> *Give ear, O heavens, and I will [sing],*
> *and let the earth hear the words of my mouth….*
> *(Deut. 31:30–32:47)*

As Israel's first ruler, Moses was their inspired hymn composer and song leader. And so was Israel's second leader.

Moses introduced Joshua as his successor in the context of singing. After God told Moses to introduce Joshua to Israel as his successor, 'Moses came and recited all the words of this song in the hearing of the people, *he and Joshua* the son of Nun' (Deut. 32:44). Joshua's first act of leadership as Moses' successor was to join him in leading praise.

It is not long before we find Joshua composing songs and leading praise on his own. In the book of Joshua, we read about Israel's initial battles in Canaan. One of these accounts tells of a miraculous intervention by God in the Aijalon Valley. God made the sun stand still and cast deadly hailstones from heaven. After describing this unparalleled victory, the narrative reports, 'At that time Joshua [sang] to the Lord…and he sang in the sight of Israel,'

Sun, stand still at Gibeon,
and moon, in the Valley of Aijalon.
And the sun stood still, and the moon stopped,
until the nation took vengeance on their enemies.
(Josh. 10:12–13)

Israel had no clear successor after Joshua's death. The period described in the Book of Judges was a time when 'every man did what was right in his own eyes,' because they lacked a king to lead them (Judg. 17:6; 18:1; 19:1; 21:25). But there were times when the people cried out to God in trouble, and he gave them a deliverer. Deborah, for example, was 'a prophetess…judging Israel' (Judg. 4:4) during a period of Canaanite oppression. She, with Barak as Israel's general, led an army of 10,000 into battle. After God gave them a mighty victory (Judg. 4), Deborah who composed a hymn for the nation's praise service. She, along with Barak, led the nation in singing it: 'Then sang Deborah and Barak the son of Abinoam on that day:'

Hear, O kings; give ear, O princes;
to the LORD I will sing;
I will make melody to the LORD,
the God of Israel…
(Judg. 5:1–31)

Eventually, Israel did obtain a king. They cried out for a king and God gave them King Saul. The sign by which God first marked out Saul for a kingly throne was musical inspiration. Samuel anointed Saul to be Israel's first king, after which Saul joined a troupe of prophets and began himself to prophesy in song with 'harp, tamborine, flute, and lyre' (1 Sam. 10:5, 9–13). We do not have any record of Saul leading the nation in praise, but it is consistent with the pattern emerging that inspired singing was a mark of Israel's rulers.

After the death of Saul, David was introduced as Israel's new king. He too was introduced through worship leadership. When Saul died, the first action of David as his successor was to teach the sons of Judah a song of lament: 'And David lamented with this lamentation over Saul and Jonathan his son, and he said it should be taught to the people of Judah…He said [or, sang]:'

> *Your glory, O Israel, is slain on your high places!*
> *How the mighty have fallen!…*
> *(2 Sam. 1:17–27)*

Directly after introducing us to David as Israel's new song leader, the Scriptures take us to the scene of his coronation as king (2 Sam. 2:1–4). Although there is no single list of the king's duties recorded in Scripture, it is becoming increasingly evident that leading in song was a regular task of Israel's ruler – even before King David.

It is King David's prolific song writing that is most familiar to us. David was anxious to prepare, in every way, for the temple which was to be built in the new capital city he had appointed (Jerusalem). As noted in our earlier study of 1 Chronicles 25, David would not write all the songs for the temple by himself. In order to magnify the grandeur of the temple and fill it with music, David created massive new orchestras and choirs, and he enlisted the help of prophetic hymnwriting teams to prepare its songs.

Having seen the close connection between song leadership and the ruler in Israel through hundreds of years before David, we can appreciate why Chronicles was careful to assure us that these new hymnists were composing 'under the hand of the king.' Israel's congregational praises were composed primarily (perhaps solely) by Israel's rulers up to that point; some arrangement for royal authorization would be needed for this introduction of additional hymnwriters. Direct oversight by David meant that all the hymns produced could still be called the 'Psalms of David' even though he now 'subcontracted' much of the writing to assistants like Asaph (Pss. 50, 73–83), Jeduthun (Pss. 39, 62, 77; maybe 89), Heman (Ps. 88), and probably others later like the sons of Korah (Pss. 42–9, 84–5, 87–8).

The preeminence of the king in Israel's praise is also evident in the performance of the Psalms. It was King David who led the people in singing the Psalms in worship. Following is one of several worship processions described to us from the time of David:

> And David and all the house of Israel were making merry before the LORD, with songs and lyres and harps and tambourines and castanets and cymbals…And David danced before the LORD with all his might. And David was wearing a linen ephod [i.e., a priestly garment indicating his sacral function, here]. So David and all the house of Israel brought up the ark of the LORD with shouting and with the sound of the horn…into the city of David (2 Sam. 6:5–16; cf., 1 Chron. 15–16).

The procession described has King David at the front, dressed in a priestly robe, leading the ascent to the temple with praises.

In biblical Israel, there were *prophets* who brought the word of God to the people in worship, there were *priests* who offered the people's sacrifices and prayers to God in worship, and there was the *king* who led the whole service. The king called the assembly to worship (e.g., 2 Sam. 6:1; 1 Chron. 15:3), he led the people in procession into God's house (2 Sam. 6:15; 1 Chron. 15:25–8), he even led in certain sacrifices and prayers during major festivals in the temple (2 Sam. 6:17; 1 Chron. 16:2).

Sacral kingship was typical of ancient Near Eastern lands, not just in Israel. The kings of the ancient world were viewed as mediators between the nation and the nation's deity, with the administration of justice as just one aspect of the king's duties. The king of Israel was therefore a *priestly*-king mediating between Yahweh and his people Israel (Ps. 110:4).

The last hymn of David's reign may have been Psalm 72. This hymn was a coronation prayer for the new king, Solomon, who would succeed David. This beautiful coronation hymn begins:

> *Give the king your justice, O God,*
> *and your righteousness to the royal son!*
> *May he judge your people with righteousness,*
> *and your poor with justice!*
> *(Ps. 72:1–2)*

Although this coronation hymn is called 'the last prayer of David' at its close (v. 20), it is also called a Psalm 'of Solomon' in its heading. Scholars have often been puzzled at how one song could be ascribed to David *and* to Solomon. While there are several possible explanations for this, we might have another transfer of power by a 'duet' in this Psalm (cf., Moses's transfer to Joshua, discussed earlier). It appears to have been cataloged in the temple library as both the last in the series of David's hymns and the first in the series of Solomon's hymns. This is, of course, speculation; but what is not speculation is that Solomon continued the practice of writing hymns for worship once he ascended to the throne (e.g., Ps. 127; cf., 1 Kings. 4:32). Likewise, other kings in David's line continued the practice.

Here is one of King Hezekiah's praise songs, recorded by the Prophet Isaiah:

> *I said, In the middle of my days*
> *I must depart [i.e., die];…*
>
> *Like a swallow or a crane I chirp;*
> *I moan like a dove.*
> *My eyes are weary with looking upwards.*

O Lord…restore me to health and make me live!
In love you have delivered my life
from the pit of destruction,
for you have cast all my sins behind your back…

The LORD will save me,
and we will play my music on stringed instruments
all the days of our lives,
at the house of the LORD.
(Isa. 38:10–20)

Hezekiah wrote this song to celebrate God's healing from an illness. This king was near death, apparently because of sin. But he cried out for mercy, and God forgave his sins and restored his health. Hezekiah composed this praise and took it to the temple for all Israel to sing with him (v. 20).

Why would God's mercy to deliver the king from death become the basis for all Israel to praise? From Adam to Jesus, Scripture shows us that God's dealings with the head of his people is a mark of his disposition toward all the people. Hezekiah's testimony about God's mercy on him became the basis for the whole congregation to praise with him. (We're getting the idea that a good singing voice must have been a prerequisite to kingship in Israel.)

There were many other songs in ancient Israel, in addition to these king-led praises. The king (and his prophetic deputies) wrote and led congregational praises, but others besides the king wrote songs for use in other contexts as well.

For instance, in Numbers 21:27–30 we find a victory song composed after a series of battles against the Amorite city of Heshbon. That song is not ascribed to Israel's ruler at the time (Moses), but is described as the work of 'ballad singers' (v. 27). Similarly, Isaiah 65:8 quotes a common laboring song. Apparently, grape harvesters in Isaiah's day would wile away the hours picking grapes by singing a song which began, 'Do not destroy it, for there is a blessing in it.'[27]

We also have songs of personal songs of praise composed by Hannah (1 Sam. 2:1–10), Jonah (Jonah 2:1–9), Mary (Luke 1:46–55), and Zechariah (Luke 1:67–79) – beautiful examples of praise, though not identified with congregational use where the king appears to have led the praises.

These and other passages scattered through the Bible demonstrate a rich culture of song throughout the history of Israel (e.g., Gen. 31:27; Judg. 11:34; 1 Sam. 18:7; Lam. 5:14; Song. 1–8; Amos 6:5; Luke 15:25; and some of the poetic portions quoted in the NT epistles may have been period songs, e.g., 1 Tim. 3:16). The ruler of Israel did not possess a monopoly on song writing. Many other songs of faith and joy appear throughout Scripture, but whenever we find examples of the congregation gathered *in public worship*, it is consistently with the songs of the ruler on their lips.

Even in the post-exilic period when there was no longer a king on the throne, the people re-organized worship, singing the songs of David and Asaph (e.g., Ezra 3:10–11). Of particular significance to Christians, we find the public praise gatherings in the New Testament also sang the Davidic Psalms – and they did so with the Son of David as their acknowledged song leader. The New Testament church saw in Jesus, the ultimate Song Leader for the church's praises.

Have you ever thought about that before? *When you sing the Psalms, you are actually singing the songs of Jesus, with Jesus as your songleader.* That is an exciting thought. It is an exciting thought celebrated in the book of Hebrews with these words: '[Jesus] … is not ashamed to call them brothers, saying,

---

27 According to their superscriptions, Psalms 57, 58 and 59 were set to a tune called 'Do Not Destroy.' Perhaps these Psalms borrowed the tune from this song mentioned in Isaiah.

"I will tell of your name to my brothers; in the midst of the congregation I will sing your praise'" (Heb. 2:11–12, quoting Ps. 22:22). It is King Jesus who takes the Davidic Psalms to his lips and sings them 'in the midst of the congregation' – and he invites us to join his songs with him.

No other praise song can do that. Fanny Crosby can offer us beautiful songs that edify our faith. William Cowper can give us words that help verbalize the awe that is in our hearts for the sacrifice of Christ. Such poets have made tremendous contributions to Christian devotion by their songs. But it is in the biblical Psalms alone that Jesus himself, our priestly king, leads our sung proclamations in the presence of the Father.

In the Gospels, Jesus often took the Psalms to his lips as his own praises. He sang Psalm 41 as his own song: 'My close friend in whom I trusted…has lifted his heel against me' (Ps. 41:9/John 13:18). He sang Psalm 118, not as a common experience of God's people but as his own experience as our true king: 'The stone that the builders rejected has become the cornerstone' (Ps. 118:22/Matt. 21:42). Jesus identified himself as the anointed king in Psalm 110: 'The LORD said to my Lord, "Sit at my right hand."' (Ps. 110:1/Mark 12:36). In these and other examples, Jesus frequently showed himself to be the Son of David by taking the Psalms of David to his lips as his own songs (e.g., Matt. 27:46/Ps. 22:1; Luke 23:46/Ps. 31:5; John 2:17/Ps. 69:9).

In fact, here is Jesus' own explanation about his relationship to the Psalms of David:

> As Jesus taught in the temple, he said, 'How can the scribes say that the Christ is the son of David? David himself, in the Holy Spirit, declared, 'The Lord said to my Lord, Sit at my right hand, until I put your enemies under your feet.' David himself calls him Lord. So how is he his son (Mark 12:35–37, quoting Ps. 110:1)?

Jesus says that David wrote Psalms for a descendant who would be greater than himself – the coming Christ. In the Holy Spirit, David understood that his songs would ultimately be taken up by the Christ.

Peter makes a similar point in his sermon at Pentecost. Peter preached from a string of Old Testament texts, including several Psalms (Pss. 16, 89, 110, 132). This is what he said concerning the Psalms:

> This Jesus, delivered up according to the definite plan and fore-knowledge of God, you crucified and killed by the hands of lawless men. God raised him up, loosing the pangs of death, because it was not possible for him to be held by it.
>
> For David says concerning him,
>
> *'I saw the Lord always before me,*
> *for he is at my right hand that I may not be shaken;*
> *therefore my heart was glad, and my tongue rejoiced;*
> *my flesh also will dwell in hope.*
> *For you will not abandon my soul to Hades,*
> *or let your Holy One see corruption.*
> *You have made known to me the paths of life;*
> *you will make me full of gladness with your presence.'*
>
> Brothers, I may say to you with confidence about the patriarch David that he both died and was buried, and his tomb is with us to this day. Being therefore a prophet, and knowing that God had sworn with an oath to him that he would set one of his descendants on his throne, he foresaw and spoke about the resurrection of the Christ, that he was not abandoned to Hades, nor did his flesh see corruption (Acts 2:25–31 quoting Ps. 16:8–11).

What an amazing statement about the Psalms! According to Peter, David wrote the Psalms 'knowing' that God had promised the Christ would come from his line. And he wrote Psalm 16 'foreseeing' the resurrection of Christ. The Psalms were born out of the experiences of David and his heirs, but David wrote with awareness of the coming Son of David who would ultimately take the Psalms to his lips as our perfect king and songleader.

From the beginning, the Psalms were composed for Jesus – as his songs. No wonder the New Testament church never set the Psalmbook aside. They took up the Psalms in great delight, singing in them with Jesus.[28]

Let me offer a word picture to anchor this principle. Imagine that a friend of yours has invited you to a concert. A famous choir is in town, and your friend bought two tickets. As you slip into your seats in the concert hall, a one hundred voice choir lines the platform before you. And the music begins. The singing is superb. It could not be better. It is such a pleasant evening, you and your friend decide to return the next week for another concert.

The next week, you return to the hall and find the same choir singing again. This time, however, a world famous tenor is going to be on the platform with them. As you sit in the audience listening, you are entranced by the beauty of the soloist's voice, surrounded majestically by the hundred-voice choir behind him. Perhaps you will come again another time to hear more.

What is the difference between these two, imagined performances? In the first, the audience is listening to the voices of a hundred singers. The song is the choir's song. In the second

28   The particular collection of 150 Psalms preserved in the canon was prepared in the post-exilic period, when there was no longer a king in Jerusalem. Arguably, the edition of the Psalter contained in the Bible is a selection of Psalms specifically chosen and compiled for the expected Messiah. (See M. LeFebvre, 'The Hymns of Christ: The Old Testament Formation of the New Testament Hymnal.')

performance, however, the audience is listening to the voice of one singer accompanied by a hundred others. But it is the one singer in front who stands under the spotlight. *His* song is being performed, and the rest join him in singing it.

In Christian worship, God is the audience of our singing. Many congregations today see themselves as that hundred-person choir singing to God. They imagine that they stand as a mass of worshipers, singing *their* songs of faith to him. That is the expectation behind modern hymns and praise songs. Modern hymns do not say, for example, 'What a friend I, Joseph Scriven, have in Jesus.' Hymnwriters compose songs for the congregation to sing as their song to God, with the song's original author and his experience disappearing from view.

This is where the Psalms are radically different. The Psalms are composed for a use like the second performance imagined above. Our divinely anointed leader, King Jesus, leads our praise. Jesus sings his own songs in his own words (composed prophetically for him). They are his praises of the Father which he calls us, as his subjects, to join him in singing. Rather than disappearing from view, we are supposed to sing in conscious identification with Jesus as our Psalm leader, and with his experience of the cross and resurrection before us.

The 18th century hymnwriting movement failed to see Christ in the Psalms, because they overlooked the church's historical realization that we need much more than praises about Jesus. Christians lost sight of the importance of singing Jesus' songs with him in worship. We need praises led by Jesus, which is what the Psalms provide. In past centuries, when Psalm singing was more common, it was the expectation of singing Jesus' songs that enlivened even the simplest Christians in singing the Psalms.

In 1692, an Anglican bishop named Samuel Patrick was among those adopting new hymns to replace Psalm singing. During one worship gathering, Bishop Patrick noted that one of the servant girls was not singing. He drew her aside afterwards to ask if she was unwell. The maid reportedly answered, 'I am well enough in health, but if you must needs know the plain truth of the matter, as long as you sung Jesus Christ's Psalms, I sang along with ye; but now you sing psalms of your own invention, you may sing by yourselves.'[29] Here was a maid who understood the difference between singing *with* Jesus and singing about him.

Deitrich Bonhoeffer understood this distinction, too. Ministering in Germany under Adolf Hitler's regime, Bonhoeffer understood what it meant to suffer for his faith. He found great strength in singing Psalms which assured him that Jesus bore his afflictions with him. Bonhoeffer wrote,

> It is the incarnate Son of God, who has borne every human weakness in his own flesh, who here [in the Psalms] pours out the heart of all humanity before God and who stands in our place and prays for us. He has known torment and pain, guilt and death more deeply than we. Therefore it is the prayer of the human nature assumed by him which comes here [in the Psalms] before God. It is really our prayer, but since he knows us better than we know ourselves and since he himself was truly human for our sakes, it is also really his prayer, and it can become our prayer only because it was his prayer.[30]

What a joy it is to have Jesus as our Prophet, speaking to us in the Scriptures in worship. What a joy it is to have Jesus as our Priest, interceding on our behalf before the throne of heaven when we pray. And what a joy to have Jesus as our King, leading us in procession and in his praises with him, into the presence of the Father.

29   M. Patrick, *Story of the Church's Song,* p113.
30   D. Bonhoeffer, *Psalms,* 20–21.

These are the two unique features of the Psalms: they are the church's only inspired hymns, and they are the church's only Christ-led hymns. In the next chapters, I want to explore these two features in closer detail. In chapters 3–4, I want to think further about what it means to sing Jesus' songs with him. In chapters 5–7, I want to look more closely at how the inspired Psalms shape our faith. My prayer is that we will rediscover the privilege and power of singing the Psalms for all they're worth.

Since the invention of the printing press, believers have had a wealth of Christian books available to read and to benefit from. Christians do well to take advantage of the practical help gained by reading quality books. But we must always continue to honor the Scriptures above all other books, because the Scriptures are divinely inspired. This principle should apply to our music as well.

There is a wealth of Christian music available for the edification of believers today. Christian music is a wonderful blessing. Enjoy the abundance of all that is available musically for your encouragement, just as you benefit from the Christian books you read. But give to the Psalms the same pride of place among your musical interests that you give to the Scriptures among your reading materials. Only the Psalms are inspired songs.

As you begin to think about the Psalms as songs to sing (not just chapters to read), think of them as *Christ's* songs, and thus exalted above all others.

3

Singing with Jesus (Part 1):
Recognizing Christ
in 'Praising Conversations'

At first glance, the coronation throne of Great Britain is not very impressive. It may have been gilt in gold at one point in its history. But any gold on it was removed long ago, leaving a blocky, bare oak chair, further marred by centuries of carved initials from choir boys and tourists. It is not much to look at, but the throne does have an impressive history. It was built in 1296 as a throne for King Edward I. It is still called 'King Edward's Chair,' and it has served as the coronation throne of English and British monarchs ever since – including the 1953 crowning of Queen Elizabeth II.[31]

The feature I find particularly striking about this throne, however, is its size. I recall standing before King Edward's Chair on a visit to Westminster Abbey some years ago, and

---

31 The only monarch not crowned in Edward's Chair was Queen Mary I. As part of her efforts to restore Catholicism to England, Mary chose to be crowned in a throne provided by the Pope. Also, Mary II was crowned on a replica of Edward's Chair.

thinking to myself, 'King Edward certainly was not that large of a man!' It is a big chair! Have you ever seen photos from Queen Elizabeth's coronation? (You can readily find them on the internet.) Even with her flowing robes, she still had plenty of room around her sitting in that seat!

I suspect that Edward deliberately designed the throne to be extra-large in order to represent the grandness of the monarch's authority. It is doubtful that Edward or any other monarch could ever 'fill' that seat.

Perhaps we might see in the physical largeness of Edward's chair, a picture of the greatness of the Davidic king described in the Psalms. Even David himself could never fulfill the perfections of the king presented in his Psalms, nor could any of his twenty-one immediate heirs in Judah. Each heir ascended, in turn, into 'David's throne,' but none 'filled' its greatness.

God covenanted to give David's throne a universal and eternal reign. 'I will make you a great name, like the name of the great ones of the earth' (2 Sam. 7:9), God said to David, referring to the aspiration of other empire-building kings of the ancient world as vain. David's throne would be the one to inherit 'a great name' over all other nations (cf., Phil. 2:9). God further swore to David, 'Your throne shall be established forever' (2 Sam. 7:16).

God's purposes for David's throne were far bigger than David himself could fulfill, and David understood this. 'Who am I,' he prayed after receiving God's promise, 'and what is my house, that you have brought me thus far?' (2 Sam. 7:18). That is more than a prayer of modesty; it was David's expression of awe at what God would accomplish through his dynasty.

David's understanding of these things influenced his penning of psalms for his heirs. David did not compose 'small psalms' that fit his own moral and sacral limitations. Nor did he write psalms with the tiny state over which he ruled in view.

David began composing Psalms for the grand vision of his dynasty, based on the huge promises which one of his heirs would accomplish.

For example, David wrote in Psalm 2:7–12,

> *I will tell of the decree,*
> *The Lord said to me,*
> *'You are my Son...*
>
> *Ask of me, and I will make the nations your heritage,*
> *and the ends of the earth your possession...'*
>
> *Now therefore, O kings, be wise;*
> *be warned, O rulers of the earth...*
> *Kiss the Son [i.e., submit to the Davidic king]...*

Also, in Psalm 72:8–17:

> *May he have dominion from sea to sea,*
> *and from the River to the ends of the earth!...*
>
> *May all kings fall down before him,*
> *all nations serve him!...*
>
> *May people be blessed in him,*
> *all nations call him blessed...*

Like the throne of King Edward, the Psalms of King David were prepared with grandness larger than the commissioning king could fill. But in David's case, a promise from God ensured that an heir would do so, one day.

The New Testament apostles understood this. Recall Peter's words to the multitudes at Pentecost. Quoting Psalm 16 (a Psalm about resurrection), Peter explained:

David says [these things] concerning him [Christ]...Being therefore a prophet, and knowing that God had sworn with an oath to him that he would set one of his descendants on his throne, he foresaw and spoke about the resurrection of the Christ, that he [Christ] was not abandoned to Hades, nor did his flesh see corruption. (Acts 2:25, 30–31; cf., Paul's words in Acts 13:36–9).

Even though they were penned centuries before Christ came, the Psalms really are the hymns of Christ.

Many psalms draw from David's personal experiences – like Psalm 3 which is tied to the time 'when he fled from Absalom his son' (Ps. 3, superscription) and Psalm 18 which celebrates 'the day when the LORD rescued him from the hand of all his enemies' (Ps. 18, superscription). But even these are more than just a recounting of David's own experiences. For instance, at the close of Psalm 18, David confesses that this personal experience of God's favor is a lesson for 'the nations' to heed concerning the victories which his heir would accomplish:

> For this I will praise you, O LORD, among the nations,
> and sing to your name.
> Great salvation he brings to his king,
> and shows stedfast love to his anointed,
> to David and his offspring forever.
> (Ps. 18:49–50)

For centuries, the people of Israel sang the Psalms in expectation of the Messiah who would 'live up to them.' When Jesus came, this was one of the things that captivated his disciples. They were amazed at the ways Jesus personified the Psalms.

John tells us about a time when Jesus entered the temple and was enraged at the marketing of animals taking place there. Jesus was not only upset, but he took bold, royal action: 'Making a whip of cords, he drove them all out of the temple...'

(John 2:15). Historically, it was always the responsibility of the Davidic king to ensure that the temple was kept pure (cf., 2 Kings 23:4). When Jesus took that responsibility upon himself, even driving out the moneychangers and their cattle, the disciples immediately recognized what was happening. 'His disciples remembered that it was written [in the Psalms], "Zeal for your house will consume me"' (John 2:17; quoting Ps. 69:9). The royal devotion to God's house, shouldered by all David's heirs in singing Psalm 69, was now being undertaken by King Jesus.

Toward the end of Jesus' earthly ministry, as he hung dying on the cross, his followers saw another Psalm of the Davidic covenant being fulfilled in him. 'At the ninth hour Jesus cried with a loud voice… "My God, my God, why have you forsaken me?"' (Mark 15:34; quoting Ps. 22:1). In his final breaths on the cross, 'he said, "It is finished," and he bowed his head and gave up his spirit' (John 19:31b; likely alluding to Ps. 22:31). The disciples saw in Jesus, there on the cross, the personification of the suffering king of Psalm 22.

All throughout his ministry, Jesus showed himself to be the king described in the Psalms – a king even greater than David. It is Jesus who fulfills every dimension of the Psalms and their covenanted roles far beyond what any of the preceding kings of the Davidic dynasty could have achieved. King Jesus is not only the next songleader of God's people in the Davidic heritage; he is the king for whom the Psalms were prepared.

In this chapter, I want to explore some of the ways this understanding of the Psalms – recognizing them as *Jesus'* Psalms – impacts the way we should sing them. First of all, I want to look more closely at the nature of the 'praising conversations' taking place when we sing Jesus' hymns with him. The Psalms are not just catechetical songs about Jesus; they are mediated praises in which Jesus is present singing with us. But these songs are more like conversations than mere monologues. In the rest of this chapter, I want to explore the nature of these Christ-led, 'praising conversations' in the Psalms.

In the next chapter, I want to look more closely at the Psalms which initially seem unlikely to be songs of Jesus. The Psalms of repentance for example: does Jesus sing songs of repentance with us? In both these chapters, my goal is to help readers sing the Psalms as the Apostles saw them: as the songs of King Jesus.

The Psalms as 'praising conversations'

Some years ago, my wife and I attended a performance of Felix Mendelssohn's *Elijah,* an oratorio about the life of Elijah. Throughout the presentation, Elijah (and the soloist who sings his part) is at the center. But there is a lot of conversation taking place between the Elijah-soloist and the other singers. For example, in the portion describing the contest on Mount Carmel (cf., 1 Kings 18:1–40), the following lines are sung:

Elijah (to the people) –

... Ye have forsaken God's commands,
and thou hast followed Baalim.
Now send, and gather to me
the whole of Israel unto Mount Carmel...
Then we shall see whose God is the Lord.

The people (to Elijah) –

And then we shall see whose God is the Lord...
Yea, and the God who by fire shall answer,
let him be God...

[At the end of the contest]

The people (to themselves) –

The fire descends from heaven!
The flames consume his offering!
Before Him upon your faces fall!
The Lord is God, the Lord is God!
O Israel hear!
Our God is one Lord,
And we will have no other gods before the Lord.

The Psalms are not stories like the *Elijah* oratorio; but they are conversations. They are conversations in which the king is always at the center, mediating our praise. But sometimes, the king speaks to the people in the Psalms. Sometimes, the king leads the people in addressing God. Sometimes, the people sing to the king, or to God about the king, or to one another before the king. The psalms are full of changing voices singing 'praising conversations' with the covenanted king at the center.

In an earlier chapter of this book, I described worship using the analogy of a choir led by a great soloist. At this point in our study, we need to nuance that illustration. The Psalms are not simply solos in which the king leads and the people 'sing along.' They are all Christ-led and Christ-centered praises, but they have a conversational design to them – not unlike the oratorio example above.

In modern musical scores, editorial notations show where one voice ends and another begins – like the notations in that portion of Mendelssohn's *Elijah* quoted above. No one sings the words, 'Elijah (to the people).' That is an editorial notation to indicate changes in voice. In ancient times, such editorial markers were not written. The singers just had to know where the voices change (cf., the unmarked changes in voice in the Song of Solomon).

There are clues in the Psalms, however, to help us discern whose voice is being lifted at various points. With attentiveness, it is possible to sing the Psalms with awareness of the 'praising conversations' through which they lead us. Let me offer several examples. But let me make two preliminary comments before turning to these examples.

First of all, Jesus leads us in singing these Psalms as our *human* king. Jesus is more than mere man; he is also fully divine. Jesus always was God (John 1:1; 8:56–8; 12:41). But the reason Jesus, already being God, took on flesh was to become the perfect man. We needed a perfect man to represent us in righteousness before God. Adam was supposed to be that man, leading the rest of the race before God; but he failed. David and his heirs could foreshadow, but could never be, the needed perfect man to lead us in righteousness to God. But Jesus, being God, humbled himself to become man in order to fulfill that role. As both God and man, then, Jesus is the mediator who reveals God to us *and* who leads men to God. It is in his role as the perfect man that Jesus intercedes for our prayers and leads our praises (Phil. 2:6–11; Heb. 2:10–18; cf., Gen. 3:15; Dan. 7:13–14; Mark 2:10, 28; Acts 17:31; Rom. 5:17).

As God, Jesus receives our worship in the Psalms. In singing these songs of worship, we offer our adoration to the entire godhead as triune Father, Son, and Holy Spirit. But, we also find that it is Jesus as our human, mediating king who is himself offering praise to God in the Psalms, and leading us in that praise. This is the marvel of Jesus' incarnation:

> For…he [Jesus] is not ashamed to call them brothers, saying, 'I will tell of your name to my brothers; in the midst of the congregation I will sing your praise'…Therefore he had to be made like his brothers in every respect, so that he might become a merciful and faithful high priest in the service of God (Heb. 2:11–18; cf., Rom. 15:9).

In the examples that follow, we will note how the Psalm singing king identifies with men, and leads men in praise of God. We do not, in any way, deny Christ's deity as the God worshiped in the Psalms as we do so. But to avail of the full blessings of his incarnation, we must also celebrate his humanity. It is with particular respect to his humanity that Jesus stands 'in the midst of the congregation,' owning our troubles and sorrows with us, to lead us in perfect praise of God.

Secondly, let me make a preliminary comment about the examples that I have chosen in what follows. We could explore the conversational nature of any of the 150 Psalms. But, for the sake of simplicity, I am going to focus on Psalms that the New Testament authors explicitly identify as Psalms of Jesus.

The New Testament quotes numerous Psalms as Psalms about Jesus.[32] Some scholars believe that only these Psalms which the New Testament specifically identifies with Jesus should be regarded as 'Messianic Psalms' (or, Psalms of Jesus). That, it seems to me, is too rigid a position. Instead, I concur with Richard Belcher that, 'The fact that [the New Testament] places some Psalms on the lips of Jesus lays the basis for understanding all the Psalms as the Psalms of Christ in his role as our Mediator.'[33]

Just as the New Testament authors quote certain portions from the Hebrew prophets, thereby showing us the ways in which all the prophecies of old pointed to Christ; as the New Testament authors quote certain portions of the Law, thereby showing us the ways in which all the Law is fulfilled in Christ; so, the New Testament writers quote from many specific Psalms, thereby showing us the way in which all the Psalms are personified in Jesus (cf., Luke 24:44).

Nevertheless, simply to set aside any possible doubt about whether the following examples really should be considered

---

32   For a conservative list, see R. Belcher, *Messiah and the Psalms,* 35–36.

33   R. Belcher, *Messiah and the Psalms,* 38.

Jesus-led Psalms, I am going to restrict myself in the following string of examples to Psalms which the New Testament specifically identify as referring to Jesus. That way, you can rest assured that these examples really are examples of Jesus-led 'praise conversations.' And I hope that, in studying these, you will grow in your appreciation for the way in which all the Psalms help us to engage our hearts in his Psalm-mediated relationship with heaven.

The Psalms as Christ-led conversations

In the first set of examples we will look at, we find **the words of the king singing to God.** In these Psalm portions, the king is the 'I' of the Psalm,[34] and God the Father is the 'you' to whom he speaks. For example, in Psalm 69:9 (applied to Jesus in John 2:17; Rom. 15:3), the king sings to God, 'Zeal for your house has consumed me.' Here, the king is the one who expresses his commitment to the holiness of God's house. When a congregation sings this psalm today, we are doing more than professing our own zeal for God's house; we are rejoicing in Jesus' devotion as the patron of God's house among us.

Another helpful example occurs in Ps. 22:22 (which Heb. 2:12 ascribes to the lips of King Jesus). The king promises to reveal God's glory to the people, singing, 'I will tell of your name to my brothers; in the midst of the congregation I will praise you.' As a congregation takes that Psalm to its lips, we are doing more than professing our own commitment to magnify the

---

34 There is a lively discussion, in scholarly circles, over the identity of the 'I' in the Psalms. Other views are regularly advanced, but it is widely accepted that the 'I' in the Psalms is the king who acts in representation of his people, since kings in the ANE typically filled this kind of representative role. Cf., Mowinckel, *Psalms in Israel's Worship,* chs 3, 7–8; J. Eaton, *Kingship and the Psalms*; J. Grant, 'The Psalms and the King.'

name of God. We are acknowledging that Christ, the Son of David, is the one who perfectly reveals the Father in the midst of his people. We are rejoicing to join him in spreading God's glory.

In many places like these, Psalm singers vocalize words that are properly the speech of Jesus to the Father, as *he* stands in our midst praising God among us.[35]

Sometimes, the Psalms give us ***words that the king sings to us.*** For instance, in Psalm 37 the songleader exhorts the congregation,

> *Fret not yourself because of evildoers;*
> *be not envious of wrongdoers!...*
> *Trust in the LORD, and do good;*
> *dwell in the land and befriend faithfulness....*
> *In just a little while, the wicked will be no more...*
> *But the meek shall inherit the land...*

It was King David who, at first, bore testimony to the faithfulness of God in that Psalm. David was the one who, through his experiences tending God's people, found that God faithfully cares for his children. He first sang that word of testimony with the gathered congregation. But Jesus has now taken that testimony to his lips (see Matt. 5:5, where Ps. 37:11 is ascribed to Jesus). In this Psalm, Jesus attests to us of heaven's faithfulness to the meek.

When a congregation sings words like these, we ought to listen to them as we sing them. They are words of comfort addressed to us. And it is not simply our fellow believers

35 Cf., Ps. 16:8–11/Acts 2:25–8, 13:35; Ps. 22:1/Matt. 27:46, Mark 15:34; Ps. 22:18/John 19:24; Ps. 31:5/Luke 23:46; Ps. 35:19/John 15:25; Ps. 40:6–7/ Heb. 10:5–7; Ps. 41:9/John 13:18; Ps. 69:4/John 15:25; Ps. 69:21/Matt. 27:34, Mark 15:23, Luke 23:36, John 19:28–30; Ps. 69:25/Acts 1:20; Ps. 102:25–6/ Heb. 1:10–12; Ps. 109:8/Acts 1:20.

(whose literal voices we hear) exhorting us. Nor is it just King David (who penned Psalm 37). Christ himself experienced the supreme faithfulness of the Father, and personally testifies to us in these lines. The king speaks to us in the Psalms (cf., Ps. 2:1–2/Acts 4:25–26; Ps. 78:2/Matt. 13:35).

So far, we have seen examples of the king singing to God, and examples of the king singing to us. In our next set of examples, the Psalms provide the congregation with words to sing to God: *the words of the people singing to God.* A great example of this is Psalm 89.

Psalm 89 was probably composed after Babylon conquered Judah. The Babylonians destroyed the temple, and they also dethroned King Zedekiah – the last son of David to reign in Jerusalem. But God had promised never to cut off the Davidic dynasty. In 2 Sam. 7:12–16, God promised David, '…I will raise up your offspring after you…When he commits iniquity, I will discipline him with the rod of men…but *my stedfast love* will not depart from him…And your house and your kingdom shall be made sure forever.' Psalm 89 celebrates that *stedfast love* of the Lord (Ps. 89:1), acknowledging God's promise to discipline rebellious sons of David (as Judah experienced under Babylon's defeat), and clinging to God's promise always to raise up a new king in David's line again.

Psalm 89 gives us lines where the congregation gathers around the promised king (in anticipation of his coming), singing to God about him:

> *Of old you spoke in a vision to your godly one*
> *[refering to the covenant God gave to David], and said,*

> *'I have…exalted one chosen from the people…*
> *I will make him the firstborn,*
> *the highest of the kings of the earth…*
> *Once for all I have sworn by my holiness;*

I will not lie to David.
His offspring shall endure forever,
his throne as long as the sun before me.
Like the moon it shall be established forever,
a faithful witness in the skies.'

In the New Testament, we discover that Jesus is that promised king whom Psalm 89 celebrates as 'the firstborn [of God], the highest of the kings of the earth' (Ps. 89:27 applied to Jesus in Rev. 1:5). The Son of David has come. He has taken up 'the throne of great dimensions.' In singing Psalm 89 today, we rejoice that so much of this Psalm's longings have been realized, and we join in its anticipation of the full and final consummation of Messiah's reign over all the earth.

In such Psalms, the king is the central figure mediating our relationship with the Father. Nevertheless, in lines like these, *the congregation sings to God.*[36]

Complementing this example where the congregation sings to God about the king, we also note Psalms which provide **words of the people singing to the king.** Psalm 110 is an interesting example. In this Psalm, the congregation sings to God *about* the king in one part, and *to* the king directly in another.

In the first half of Psalm 110 (vv. 1–4), the people sing *to the king*, who has been exalted to a throne at the right hand of God:

The LORD [God] said to my Lord [the king]:
'Sit at my right hand,
until I make your enemies your footstool.'
The LORD sends forth from Zion

---

36 Cf., Ps. 8:2/Matt. 21:16; Ps. 8:4–6/Heb. 2:6–8; Ps. 118:26/Matt. 21:9, 23:39, Mark 11:9, Luke 13:35, 19:38, John 12:13; Ps. 132:11/Acts 2:30.

your [i.e., the king's] mighty scepter.
Rule in the midst of your enemies!
Your [i.e., the king's] people will offer themselves
freely [in your service]...

Notice how the opening verse quotes the instruction of God to his favored king. Then, based on that word, the congregation begins to sing to the king, praising his mighty scepter and certain victories. These opening verses lead the congregation in singing to the anointed king. At verse 5, however, the Psalm switches to address God about the king:[37]

The Lord [the king] is at your [God's] right hand;
he [the king] will shatter kings on the day of his wrath.
He [the king] will execute judgment among the nations...

It is King Jesus who is at the center of this Psalm. As Jesus explained in Luke 20:41–3, David never fulfilled the greatness of this Psalm himself. David wrote it with his greater heir in mind. This is another Psalm which the apostles recognized as being about Jesus (Matt. 22:44; Mark 12:36; Luke 20:42; Acts 2:34; 1 Cor. 15:25; Eph. 1:22; Heb. 1:13; 5:6; 7:17, 21; 10:12). In the course of our singing Psalm 110 today, we enter into a conversation speaking both to Christ (vv. 1–4) and to the Father about Christ (vv. 5–7). The first half of this Psalm, therefore, illustrates lines which the congregation sings to the king. (Cf., Ps. 45:6–7/Heb. 1:8–9; Ps. 68:18/Eph. 4:8.)

Let me note one further example. In addition to the various 'directions in conversation' already described, the Psalms also provide ***words the people sing to themselves***.

---

37   There are no editorial notations to tell us about this change of audience. Nonetheless, vv. 1–4 are addressed *to* the one called 'Lord' (*Adonai*), who is 'at the Lord's right hand,' while vv. 5–7 are talking *about* the one called 'Lord' (*Adonai*) and are addressed to the one 'on whose right hand' *Adonai* sits.

There is a good example of this in Psalm 118. Jesus quoted this Psalm as about himself the week before his crucifixion, saying, 'Have you never read in the Scriptures, "The stone that the builders rejected has become the cornerstone; this was the Lord's doing, and it is marvelous in our eyes"?' (Matt. 21:42; quoting Ps. 118:22–23; cf., Mark 12:10–11, Luke 20:17, Acts 4:11, 1 Pet. 2:7). Jesus is 'the stone the builders rejected' in Psalm 118.

Now look at that portion in its original context in Psalm 118:

> *The stone that the builders rejected*
> *has become the cornerstone.*
> *This is the Lord's doing;*
> *it is marvelous in our eyes.*
> *This is the day that the Lord has made;*
> *let us rejoice and be glad in it.*

In this portion of Psalm 118, the people are exhorting one another. The congregation exalts in the marvelous work God is doing 'in our eyes' with the foundation stone rejected by men. This is an example of the people singing to one another within the 'praising conversations' of Jesus' Psalms.

Psalm 118 actually illustrates several aspects of the 'praising conversations' we've been exploring. In the first two parts of the Psalm (vv. 1–4, and vv. 5–20), the songleading king sings to the people (king → us). In the first part, the king calls the people to praise with him:

> *Oh give thanks to the Lord, for he is good;*
> *for his stedfast love endures forever!*
> *Let Israel say, 'His stedfast love endures forever.'*
> *Let the house of Aaron say, 'His stedfast love endures forever.'*
> *Let those who fear the Lord say, 'His stedfast love endures forever.'*

In the second part (vv. 5–20), the king testifies to the people about the certain victory God will give to him. Even though mighty foes surround and defy our king's work, he is confident of complete victory because he is a king in perfect and loving relationship with God:

> *The LORD is on my side; I will not fear*
> *What can man do to me?...*
> *I shall look in triumph on those who hate me...*
> *All nations surrounded me...*
> *I shall not die, but I shall live,*
> *and recount the deeds of the LORD.*

In verse 21 of the Psalm, the king turns his address toward God the Father in a sung prayer (king → God):

> *I thank you that you have answered me*
> *and have become my salvation.*

This ends those portions of the Psalm where the king's voice is at the fore. In the next part of the Psalm (vv. 22–24), the congregation responds to the king's faith with our own song of faith. First, the congregation sing to one another (us → one another), delighting at the marvelous work God is doing in our suffering yet victorious king:

> *The stone that the builders rejected*
> *has become the cornerstone...*
> *This is the day that the LORD has made;*
> *let us rejoice and be glad in it.*

In verse 25, the congregation turns its address toward God (us → God) in a sung prayer which parallels that of the king (v. 21):

Save us, we pray, O Lord!
O Lord, we pray, give us success!

The closing verses of the Psalm (vv. 26–29) reflect rapidly changing voices, as the congregation praises the king (us → king) and exhorts one another (us → one another), and the king rejoins the song, exalting in God (king → God) and closes the Psalm with the same call to the congregation with which he started it (king → us):

The congregation (to the king)[38] –

Blessed is he who comes in the name of the Lord!
We bless you in the name of the Lord!

The congregation (to one another) –

The Lord…has made his light to shine upon us.
Bind the festal sacrifice…[on] the altar!

The king (to God) –

You are my God, and I will give thanks to you;
you are my God; I will extol you.

The king (to the congregation; cf., v. 1) –

Oh give thanks to the Lord, for he is good;
for his stedfast love endures forever!

38 Note that this portion, which the congregation sings to the king, is the portion which Matthew quotes from the congregation's singing as Jesus entered Jerusalem on a donkey the week before his crucifixion (Matt. 21:9).

Psalm 118 illustrates the rich conversations that the Psalms facilitate. This 'conversational praise' is one of the unique characteristics that sets these hymns apart from the modern hymns people write. It is also one of the reasons why we ought to relearn the blessings of singing entire Psalms – following entire 'conversations' through from beginning to end – rather than lifting choruses or small portions out of context.

In addition to the relationships we've explored above (king → God; king → us; us → God; us → king; us → one another), there are also Psalms where God sings to us (God → us; e.g., Ps. 89:20/Acts 13:22), where God addresses the king (God → king; e.g., Ps. 2:7/Acts 13:33), and even points where we, the king, or God address the world around us (God, king, or us → world; e.g., Ps. 2:10–11/Phil. 2:10, 12).

In these 'praising conversations,' every direction of the covenant relationship centered around Christ is exercised. In their original performances in the temple, it is likely that parts of the Psalms were literally sung by the king, with other parts sung by the congregation. Perhaps the king also would have sung the words of God to the people, or perhaps a prophet would have filled that role. It is not clear exactly how the various changes in address might have been represented in the original singing of these Psalms. But the dynamic of conversation is very much a part of them.

When we sing the Psalms today, we do not have Christ audibly singing his parts in our midst. Nor does God sing, audibly, in our midst. Nevertheless, when the congregation gathers for worship in the name of Christ, he promises to be in our midst with us (Matt. 18:20); and, when the congregation sings these Psalms of David's greater son in worship, Christ sings in them before God with us.

Remember, all of the examples I have given above (including the references along the way) are Psalms that the New Testament specifically identifies with Jesus. The New Testament teaches us to see Christ in the 'praising conversations' of the Psalms. Even though he does not make his voice heard, literally, in our midst, in the Psalms the voice of Jesus sings with his people.

All this switching of voices in the Psalms probably sounds complicated. I suppose it is. But it is that complexity which makes the Psalms so vibrant and, indeed, relational. We ought not ignore this feature of the Psalms just because we are not used to it. And as complicated as changes in voice sound when we analyze specific Psalms, the principle is not that difficult once we take up the Psalms and just sing them.

The Psalms are designed to be sung with delight and simplicity. Just as an automobile is complicated 'under the hood,' so these Psalms are doing a lot of work on our behalf in the way they are designed. It is helpful when driving a car to have some understanding of what is going on under the hood, but you don't have to be a mechanic to drive. Likewise, when singing the Psalms, it is not necessary to stop and figure out exactly what direction the covenant conversation is moving at this point or that point in the Psalm.

In some places, the voice that is singing will be clear; at other points, it is not so obvious. And frankly, one of the points of singing with Jesus is that he takes up our troubles in his voice, and he invests his victories into ours. In other words, even when *the king* is the 'I' of the Psalm, saying, 'I shall not die, but I shall live, and recount the deeds of the LORD' (Ps. 118:17), you and I are supposed to claim that hope as our own, as well – making ourselves the 'I' in that claim with Jesus.

There is an old Jewish saying, 'All that David said in his Book of Psalms applies to himself, to all Israel, and to all the ages.'[39] That is exactly right. David wrote of his own experiences of God's grace, but his words are also about the experiences of all

---

39   From the *Midrash Tehillim* on Ps. 18.

God's people with him. And they are praises for the promised king (the Christ) and his people (his church) through the ages.

So, having just endeavored to clarify the lines of conversation taking place in the Psalms, I'm now blurring them again. But just a bit. The point of Psalm singing is not to engage in textual analysis while singing; but, it will make your singing so much more meaningful and rewarding, if you sing them with a growing level of awareness of the conversations in which they lead us. When you take up these hymns from the Son of David, you are entering into an exercise of your covenant relationship as believers. Jesus is meeting with you there, and leading you into a 'praising conversation' with God, with one another, and indeed before the world.

Singing with this awareness will make Psalmody richer and more fruitful. Paul himself exhorts this conversational approach to our singing: 'Let the word of Christ dwell in you richly [i.e., the words of the king in our midst], teaching and admonishing one another in all wisdom [i.e., the people addressing one another], singing psalms and hymns and spiritual songs, with thankfulness in your hearts to God [i.e., singing with Christ unto God]' (Col. 3:16).

A great way to sharpen your alertness to the 'praising conversations' in the Psalms, is to do personal study in several Psalms, looking for the ways in which the voices change through them. Don't try to cover all the Psalms in this kind of study (unless you are really ready to take on a mammoth project!). Nevertheless, pick three or four of your favorite Psalms, and use your private devotional times over the next week or so to carefully read them, noting the implicit or explicit speaker(s) and audience(s) indicated through them. A good commentary on the Psalms will be a helpful resource in this study.

Begin to sing the Psalms, alerted to the general principle that the Psalms are relationship exercises – 'praising conversations' between you, other believers, and the Triune God – all centered in the mediation of Christ.

4

SINGING WITH JESUS (PART 2):
CHRIST IN THE PSALMS OF REPENTANCE AND
DAVIDIC EVENTS

Margaret Wilson was a young lady living in Scotland during the period known as the 'Killing Times.' From 1680 until 1688, King Charles II and, after him, King James VII sent soldiers through the south of Scotland to round up members of 'unauthorized' churches (informally called the Covenanters).

Margaret was 18 years old when she was arrested. She was tied to a stake in the waters of the Solway Firth at low tide and left to drown as the tide came in. The hope of her captors was that she would recant as the waters rose. But instead of recanting, she began to sing Psalm 25, starting with verse 7:

> *Let not the errors of my youth*
> *nor sins, remember'd be:*
> *In mercy, for thy goodness' sake,*
> *O Lord, remember me...*[40]

---

40   From the Scottish metrical version.

Margaret prepared herself to meet God by singing a Psalm of repentance. Repentance is not a popular topic, but the Psalms of repentance are part of the Psalter and a valuable aid to our walk with God.

In this book, we have been looking at the presence of Christ in the Psalms, as the one who leads us in singing them. Was Jesus there, with Margaret, leading her in this Psalm of repentance? We readily accept that Jesus was there to *hear* her repentance, but are we to understand that Jesus *sings* even such a song as that with us?

In this chapter, I want to look at two, seemingly difficult aspects of finding Christ's voice in the Psalms. The first is this matter of the Psalms of repentance. After that, we'll look at the connection of many Psalms with specific experiences in David's life.

Christ in the Psalms of repentance

People often find the Psalms of repentance the most difficult to sing as *Jesus'* words. Afterall, he was sinless. How could he ever sing, 'Let not the errors of my youth, nor sins, remember'd be'?

That is an understandable question. In fact, it is an issue John the Baptist struggled with as well (Matt. 3:1–17).

As the voice of one crying in the wilderness, 'Prepare the way of the Lord,' John the Baptist called sinners to repent. He warned that Messiah would bring righteousness to a sinful world, calling sin to account. He urged people to get ready by a baptism of repentance.

Then he came: the Messiah was there, walking along the shore toward John. But to John's surprise, the Messiah himself came down into the water for the baptism of repentance. 'John would have prevented him,' Matthew reports. John actually wanted to stop Jesus from coming into the water! 'I need to be baptized by you,' John argued, 'and do you come to me?'

This was astounding to John, that the Messiah would submit to repentance! No, he thought, it is I who must repent, and all these people, not Jesus!

But Jesus responded to John with one of the most profound statements about the nature of his mediation: 'Let it be so now, for thus it is fitting for us to fulfill all righteousness' (Matt. 3:14). This is the way that I come to bring righteousness to men, Jesus was saying, by identifying with my penitent people. Jesus came to be 'the Lamb of God who takes away the sin of the world' (John 1:29; cf., Isa. 53:10–12). Jesus even owns the sins of his people, to lead them in repentance.

The Apostle Paul marvels at this truth in his letter to the Corinthians. 'For our sake [God] made him to be sin who knew no sin, so that in him we might become the righteousness of God' (2 Cor. 5:21; cf., Gal. 4:4). Jesus never sinned, but he identifies with us as our Mediator even to the point of taking our sin and its guilt upon himself. As John Calvin wrote in one place, 'This was the reason of his silence at the judgment-seat of Pilate, though he had a just defense to offer; [because of his] having become answerable for *our* guilt…'[41]

The Psalms that lead us in repentance are among the most rewarding Psalms to sing with Jesus. They are the hymns which show how closely Christ identifies with us in our deepest need. And they give us songs whereby we can confess our own sins before the Father, and do so knowing without a doubt that Jesus truly does stand with us to intercede even in our repentance.

Let's look at an example. Psalm 40 is a Psalm of repentance which the New Testament book of Hebrews specifically places on the lips of Jesus:

---

41 Calvin, *Isaiah*, 8.119. (Italics added.) Cf., R. Belcher, *Messiah and the Psalms*, 87–88.

Consequently, when Christ came into the world, he said [or, sang]: 'Sacrifices and offerings you have not desired, but a body you have prepared for me; in burnt offerings and sin offerings you have taken no pleasure. Then I said, "Behold, I have come to do your will, O God, as it is written of me in the scroll of the book."'

When he said above, 'You have neither desired nor taken pleasure in sacrifices and offerings and burnt offerings and sin offerings' (these are offered according to the law), then he added, 'Behold, I have come to do your will.' He abolishes the first in order to establish the second. And by that will we have been sanctified through the offering of the body of Jesus Christ once for all. (Heb. 10:5–10).

In the portion of Psalm 40 that Hebrews 10 cites, Christ speaks of himself as being, in his own body, the sacrifice foreshadowed in all the ritual sacrifices of the law. New Testament-era Judaism had come to expect a Messiah who would conquer by killing others (e.g., the Romans), but the writer of Psalm 40 understood that the Messiah would bring salvation from sin by offering his own life as a sacrifice.

Adam had learned this in the Garden of Eden, when God announced that 'the seed of the woman' would take the bruise of sin on himself (Gen. 3:15). Abraham learned this hope when God told him to take his heir (Isaac) up on the mountain as a sacrifice (Gen. 22:1–14). Isaac was not slain (he could never have atoned for others' sins, himself). But through that experience, Abraham learned that there would be an heir one day who would become that sacrifice. As Genesis 22:14 explains, 'Abraham called the name of that place, "The Lord will provide"; as it is said to this day, "On the mount of the Lord it [or, he] shall be provided."' One day, the heir who would die for the people would come.

Isaiah 53 is probably a meditation on that Genesis 22:14 promise to Abraham. Isaiah also speaks of the coming heir

who must himself be the sacrifice, taking on himself the sins
of the people:

> *He was despised and rejected by men;*
> *a man of sorrows, and acquainted with grief...*
> *Surely he has borne our griefs*
> *and carried our sorrows...*
> *He was wounded for our transgressions;*
> *he was crushed for our iniquities...*
> *and the LORD laid on him the iniquity of us all.*

In the days of the New Testament apostles, many of the Jews had
focused on the prophetic announcements of Messiah's victory,
feeding their hopes of freedom from Roman oppression. But
they overlooked the many passages in the Old Testament
which spoke of Messiah's suffering. A major emphasis of Paul's
missionary work in the synagogues of his day was to re-educate
his hearers on the Old Testament teachings that 'the Christ
must suffer' (Acts 17:3; 26:23; cf., Peter's sermon in Acts 3:18).

Psalm 40 is a hymn originating in Old Testament worship
that shows David's understanding this need, and that the
sacrifices in the law would be fulfilled in the body of that
coming king. David could not be that sacrifice, himself. But he
went ahead to compose a Psalm in which he professed, in his
office as king, to be that very sacrifice. He did so 'knowing that
God had sworn with an oath to him that he would set one of
his descendants on his throne' to fulfill the covenanted duties
of Israel's mediatorial king (Acts 2:30). Hebrews 10 shows us
that, 'When Christ came into the world,' he came singing even
this Psalm – fulfilling its profound dimensions.

Along with this profession of the king offering himself as the
true sacrifice, Psalm 40 also gives us lines in which the king
owns our sins and leads us in repenting for them. The Psalm,
in the king's voice, continues to say:

As for you, O Lord, you will not restrain
your mercy from me...

For evils have encompassed me beyond number;
my iniquities have overtaken me,
and I cannot see;
they are more than the hairs of my head;
my heart fails me...

It cannot be denied that the first part of Psalm 40 are the words of Jesus. Hebrews 10 explicitly tells us so. But some commentators are wary of regarding these lines of repentence in the same Psalm as being led in the voice of Christ. For example, James Montgomery Boice wrote in his commentary:

> Is this a messianic psalm? Saint Augustine, Charles Haddon Spurgeon, William L. Pettingill, and Harry A. Ironside thought so, in large part because verses 6 and 7 are applied to Jesus Christ in the New Testament. But this is an unnecessary and misleading assumption for the psalm as a whole. The mere fact that the psalmist confesses his sin in verse 12 warns us against applying everything in the psalm to Jesus Christ.[42]

While this kind of thinking is rooted in a right reverence for Christ's personal sinlessness, it is an approach to the Psalms that fails to grasp the significance of Jesus' mediatorial kingship. Though himself sinless, he truly does take our guilt upon himself – and he leads us in repenting for it over his sacrifice. To quote again the words of Paul: 'For our sake [God] made him to be sin who knew no sin...' (2 Cor. 5:21). That is grace!

As Boice noted, Augustine is among those who see the entire Psalm 40 as words of Christ. Note how Augustine explains Jesus singing repentence in this Psalm:

---

42   J. Boice, *Psalms 1–41*, p347.

If haply any one asks, what person is speaking in this Psalm? I would say briefly, 'It is Christ.' But as ye know, brethren, and as we must say frequently, Christ sometimes speaks…in the Person of our Head [i.e., as our Mediatorial King]…He deigned to become our Head; to become 'the Head of the Body,' by taking of us that flesh in which He should die for us…

He then sometimes speaks in the name of our Head…For both when He said, 'I was an hungred, and ye gave Me meat,' (Matt. xxv. 35). He spoke on behalf of His members, not of Himself: and when He said, 'Saul, Saul, why persecutest thou Me?' (Acts ix. 4.) the Head was crying on behalf of its members: and yet He did not say, 'Why dost thou persecute My members?' but, 'Why persecutest thou Me?'…

Such is the love of Christ. What is there can be compared to this? This is the thing on account of which 'He hath put a hymn in our mouth,' and this He speaks on behalf of His members.[43]

In this book, I am agreeing with Augustine that the Psalms are hymns which Jesus puts in our mouths, and in them he speaks with us. But he speaks in the Psalms as our representative head – our mediatorial king. The Psalms of repentance are no exception to this mediation. Jesus never sinned, but as our mediator, he took personal responsibility for our sins.

The only way we can properly repent of our sins before God is by repenting in the name and sacrifice of Jesus Christ. That is not just theory, the Psalms of repentance give us precious prayers to actually do just that: to repent in the name of Jesus who willingly owns our sins and pays for them on our behalf. Of course, we can repent in private prayer on our own too. But, in times of corporate repentance in worship, the Psalms give us king-mediated songs for repentance.

---

43   Augustine, *Psalms,* in: *NPNF* 1.8, 120–21.

Christ in the Psalms of Davidic events

We have been learning to see Jesus as the true Psalm-leader. From Psalm 1 to Psalm 150, we sing the Psalms (including repentance Psalms) as 'praising conversations' mediated by Christ. Before concluding this part of our study of Psalm singing, however, we need to step back and reflect on the clear connections between so many of the Psalms and specific, historical experiences in the life of King David – and others of his heirs and Psalm-writing assistants.

In the Hebrew Psalter, there are fourteen Psalms with superscriptions tying them to events in David's life. Here they are, listed in chronological order according to the order of the indicated experiences:

Psalm	Event in David's life	Reference
59	when Saul sent men and they watched the house to kill him	1 Sam. 19:11
56	when the Philistines seized him in Gath	1 Sam. 21:10–11
34	when he feigned madness before Abimelech ...	1 Sam. 21:12–15
57	when he fled from Saul in the cave	1 Sam. 22:1 (or 24:3)
142	when he was in the cave	1 Sam. 22:1 (or, 24:3)
63	when he was in the wilderness of Judah	1 Sam. 22:5 (or, 23:14–15; 2 Sam. 15–17)
52	when Doeg the Edomite ... said to Saul, 'Is not David ... among us?'	1 Sam. 22:9–19
54	when the Ziphites went and told Saul, 'Is not David hiding among us?'	1 Sam. 23:19

Psalm	Event in David's life	Reference
7	concerning Cush, a Benjamite	uncertain? (cf., 1 Sam. 23:25)
30	at the dedication of the house [of David?]	2 Sam. 2:3–4
60	when he fought ... and Joab smote 12,000 of Edom ...	2 Sam. 8:1–14
51	when Nathan the prophet came to him, after ... Bathsheba	2 Sam. 11–12
3	when he fled from Absalom his son	2 Sam. 15–17
18	in the day that the LORD delivered him from all his enemies ...	2 Sam. 22

In the Psalms, there are many references to personal experiences which David and other Psalm writers had. This fact might pose another difficulty for seeing Jesus in the Psalms. It is easy to see David in these Psalms, but why are they so thoroughly filled with David's life if we are supposed to find his greatest heir in them? To ask the same question another way: If David really was composing his Psalms with the coming Christ in mind, why did he write them with so much of his own voice and experiences in them?

That is a fair question. Let me use an illustration to help introduce its answer. Suppose that a foreign tourist visiting America came up to an American on the street, and asked him to explain what the President of the United States does. How would the American answer? Most likely, he would talk about the various roles which Presidents fulfill: the President is the head of the government, directing each of the various departments in their activities; he is the Commander in Chief of the military; he appoints justices to the Supreme Court; and so on. Typically, the way we explain the office of the Presidency is by describing, in abstract terms, its various functions.

Not so in the ancient world. The way a question like that would be answered (if we were to answer that question in an 'Old Testament style'), would be with stories. 'Let me tell you about George Washington,' we might say. And then, 'Let me further tell you about Abraham Lincoln ... and Franklin Delano Roosevelt ... and Ronald Reagan,' and so forth. Through concrete examples of historical Presidents (rather than abstract descriptions of their roles), we would build a series of stories that, altogether, describe what the ideal President looks like.

This, really, is what the Book of Genesis does, showing us what 'a true member of Israel' looks like by showing us the accumulated stories of the Patriarchs. It is also what the Old Testament historical narratives do, showing in the stories of the judges and kings and prophets and priests (both positive and negative) what Israel needs in the ideal king and prophet and priest.

In this spirit, the Psalms often describe the personal experiences of David and his heirs by which the ideals of the rightful King of Israel are demonstrated.

In Psalm 56, for instance, we are invited to remember the story of David's imprisonment by the Philistines in Gath (1 Sam. 21:10–15). While he was running from King Saul, David tried to hide with the Philistines. But the Philistines readily recognized him as the military hero of Israel who had killed Goliath (the soldier giant who had, himself, come from Gath). David was alarmed upon being found out, and he 'pretended to be insane in their hands' (v. 13). Rather than looking like the great military hero the Philistines thought he was, this man now appeared to Achish, king of Gath, like a madman. As a result, Achish dismissed David as harmless. And David, suprisingly, escaped.

Psalm 56 (which is tied to that event) tells us nothing about David's 'playing insane' or anything like that. But it does invite us into David's inner thoughts as he realized the grave danger he was in, and then the deliverance God gave him. With Saul seeking to kill him across the border in Israel, and with the Philistines now 'onto him' here in Gath, David had no place of refuge. But, as he testified in that Psalm,

> *In God, whose word I praise,*
> *in God I trust;*
> *I shall not be afraid.*
> *What can flesh do to me?*
> *(Ps. 56:4)*

And indeed, the Psalm ends,

> *You have delivered my soul from death,*
> *yes, my feet from falling,*
> *that I may walk before God*
> *in the light of life. (v. 13)*

Through a concrete experience in the life of David, with a hymn that matches the dangers and promises at the core of David's own experience, the Psalm draws from that experience of David a lesson on God's relationship with our mediatorial king.

Jesus himself, in his humanity, never faced the Philistines at Gath. He never played the madman as David did (although he, too, was charged with being insane by his adversaries; John 10:20). Nevertheless, in David's experience of God's deliverance, even when kings on every side (Israel and Philistia) were threatening him, the peace that David found provided a lesson on God's faithfulness to the Davidic throne.

William Binnie, a Reformed Presbyterian minister in nineteenth century Scotland, wrote an 1867 article on David's poetical labors. He explained:

> Through Nathan [David] learned that the Promised Seed, the Hope of Israel, was to be born of his family and to be the heir of his throne. He was thus taught to regard himself as a man who had been raised up to foreshadow his Lord…Thus he was put in a position to write not only psalms that were strictly prophetical of Christ, but a multitude of others which, although in some sense applicable to himself and his people, looked beyond him and them to the Person and Kingdom of the Son.[44]

Throughout the Psalms, there are references to experiences in David's life that Jesus does not directly share (esp., the sins of David, as articulated in the superscription for Ps. 51). Nonetheless, this does not contradict the apostolic teaching that the Psalms were prepared for Jesus. David and the other Psalm writers learned, through concrete experiences of God's faithfulness, the nature of Christ's devotion to the covenanted throne of Israel. All of these lessons are preserved in songs prepared for the Son of David who would really personify those ideals. That anticipated Messiah has come, and his name is Jesus. And the Psalms are his songs.

Conclusion: Finding Christ in the Psalms

Many modern hymns are written *to* Jesus, or are written *about* Jesus. The Psalms also include portions addressed to Christ and many lines about him. But in all the Psalms (and only in the Psalms) we have words *of* Christ to sing *with* him. Finding Jesus in the Psalms is not simply about the prophecies of his work in this line or in that line. We find Jesus in the Psalms by hearing his voice leading our praise in every line.

When we sing songs like 'Amazing Grace' or 'How Deep the Father's Love For Us,' we don't sing them with their authors –

---

44   W. Binnie, 'David, the Sweet Psalmist of Israel,' p339.

John Newton and Stuart Townend, respectively. Neither Newton nor Townend are present in our services – and neither of these men can (or would presume to!) mediate our acceptance before God. Such songs can speak about Jesus, but they cannot give us the voice of Jesus.

But Jesus is present with his people in worship. As our Prophet, he speaks to us in the Scriptures preached. As our Priest, he intercedes for us in the prayers offered in his name. And as our King, he mediates our entrance into the presence of the Father, a blessing we embrace as we sing his Psalms with him.

Historically, the Psalms were treasured by the Church because they are the hymns of Jesus. The time has come for us to recover a passion for singing, not just about Jesus – but singing with him.

In the historic liturgies of the church, worship usually begins with a time of repentance. Drawing upon the patterns taught in Scripture, where even from Old Testament times men approached God only with a sacrifice, congregations have often made it a practice of beginning worship with repentance (Cf., T. Johnson, *Leading in Worship*, 15).

Singing one of the Psalms of repentance is a fitting way to approach worship reverently, either in a congregational setting or in private devotions. Consider using the following Psalms of repentance in your worship: Psalms 6:1–5; 25:8–11; 32:1–6; 39:1–8; 40:11–16; 41:4–10; 51:1–12; 79:8–9; 80:1–3; 81:1–16; 85:1–4; 106:1–7; 130:1–3; 139:1–3, 23–24; 141:1–5; 143:1–8).

5

Confusion and Glory (part 1):
Using the Psalms
as They're Meant to Be Used

Nails are efficiently designed for what they do. With the forceful swing of a hammer, your nail will sink through one board and secure it to the board behind.[45]

Screws, likewise, are well-designed for their purpose. Although similar to the nail in many ways, the screw has the added feature of spiraled thread running up its shaft, and a notched head. But the screw's distinct design requires a distinct action. It must be *turned* into the surface with a screwdriver, not pounded like a nail. (Can you imagine the splintering mess which would result if a builder started hammering screws into two-by-fours?) For the screw to function at its best, it must be used according to its design.

---

45 This chapter has appeared in earlier forms in: M. LeFebvre, 'Torah-Meditation and the Psalms' ; M. LeFebvre, 'Torah-Meditation in Song.'

The same is true of the Psalms. The ancient hymns of Israel (the Psalms) are as different from modern hymns as screws are from nails. Not only do the Psalms lead us in praise in the train of our Mediatorial King, but they also lead us in a very different 'method' of praise than modern church songs. Although the Psalms serve in generally the same capacity as modern hymns (to praise God), they are different in how they function within the heart as they stir that praise of God.

To be specific: modern hymns are typically designed to prompt praise through declaration. For instance, one of Martin Luther's well-loved favorites, 'A Mighty Fortress,' declares,

> *A mighty fortress is our God,*
> *a bulwark never failing;*
> *Our helper he, amid the flood*
> *of mortal ills, prevailing...*

In that beautiful song, Luther calls Christians to declare the stedfast protection of God. Although there is a foe who 'seeks to work us woe,' we need not fear 'for God hath willed his truth to triumph' – and, indeed, to triumph even 'through us.' Luther's song is a *declaration* of God's faithful victory in his church.

The Psalms are different, however. Although the Psalms are full of declarations of praise, they also include doubts, contradictions, problems, and expectations of judgment – all of which feel very awkward to sing if we sing the Psalms within the expectations of modern hymnody (rather like the awkwardness of driving screws with a hammer). But this is part of the distinct design of the biblical hymns; and, it is a distinct design which calls for a distinct expectation and 'heart activity' as we sing them.

It is the nature of that 'heart motion' behind our singing of the Psalms that is the subject of this chapter. And it is my thesis, in this chapter, that in the Psalms, praise is the expected outcome, but meditation is the underlying activity which we undertake in Psalm singing. Unlike modern church songs which are primarily about 'getting right to the point' and declaring praise, the Psalms are designed to help people who don't always feel like praising begin by meditating on the mess the world is in, and only through a full and robust process of meditation, to come out with praise.

Praise is so vital an outcome from psalmody that we use the word 'Psalms' (lit., 'Praises') to describe them. In Hebrew, the volume is called *Tehilim,* meaning 'praises,' and in Greek it is called *Psalmoi,* which likewise indicates songs of joy and praise. But even a cursory reading of the Psalms reveals that they are not all hymns of declarative praise. There is a lot of moaning and groaning going on in the Psalms. The book is called 'Praises,' not because each individual hymn contained in it is joyful. The book is called 'Praises' because the nature of the whole collection is to carry us from sorrow to praise.

We use a similar method for naming streets in our culture. I live on the edge of Indianapolis, just south of another city called Lafayette. One of the major north-south routes on my side of Indianapolis is a street called, 'Lafayette Rd.' It is called Lafayette, not because I live in the city of Lafayette (I live in Indianapolis), but it is so named because, if you follow that road where it leads, you will end up in the city of Lafayette.

In the same way, the book of Psalms is so named because these are sung meditations, which meet us in the 'city of confusion and trouble' where we live and, if we follow them where they take us, they carry us ultimately to the 'city of praise and rejoicing.' This is true of each Psalm within its own compass on the small scale (each Psalm, generally, tends to lift us from questions to answers). This is also true of the Psalmbook as a whole. In fact, the Early Church Father Gregory of Nyssa, wrote a book in the fourth century to describe how the Psalter carries us from the sorrow of living in a place of ungoldy, sinners, and scorners (in Ps. 1) to the heavenly assembly of joy (in Ps. 150).[46]

The fact that the Psalter is a collection that lifts us to praise, but is itself full of much that is not praise, highlights the importance of rediscovering the use for which they were designed. Singing them and expecting 'to declare praise' like modern hymns tend to do, is a bit like hammering with a set of screws in your hand. These Psalms require a different kind of 'heart motion' as we sing them – meditation rather than declaration.

A great example, for illustrating the meditational nature of the Psalms, is Psalm 73. It is a Psalm full of struggles. In its header, it is called 'A Psalm of Asaph' (one of the composers we talked about in chapter two of this book). We cannot know whether this Psalm arose out of the experiences of Asaph, or of the king for whom he wrote, or of other Israelites whose common struggles this Psalm was composed to address. By its inclusion in the royal hymnal, though, we are comforted that it is ultimately our mediatorial king (Jesus) who takes it up, who identified with our struggles in his own humanity, and who leads us through those struggles to victorious praise.

The Psalm opens with a grand declaration of God's goodness: 'Truly God is good to Israel, to those who are pure in heart' (v. 1). This is a truth that we learn from God's Word. Throughout the Scriptures, we are taught to trust in God's

46   Cf., Gregory of Nyssa's discerning work on the arrangement of the Psalms, in which he shows how the whole book, 'by a systematic, natural order,' carries the singer along the path 'to attain blessedness.' (Gregory of Nyssa, *Inscriptions of the Psalms,* 24.) Modern scholars also recognize the movement of the Psalms from sorrow to joy, with an eschatological direction. Cf., B. Childs, *Introduction to the OT,* 518, 522; G. Wilson, *Editing of the Psalter,* 208–14; C. Westermann, *Praise and Lament,* 258; W. Brueggemann, 'Bounded by Obedience and Praise.'

faithful goodness to his people, and to devote ourselves to holiness. But no sooner than Psalm 73 makes this assertion, it invites questions (vv. 2–3):

> *But as for me, my feet had almost stumbled,*
> *my steps had nearly slipped.*
> *For I was envious of the arrogant,*
> *when I saw the prosperity of the wicked.*

I came 'this close' to abandoning my faith in God's goodness, our Psalm-leader leads us in confessing. First of all, those whom God calls wicked are actually the ones who seem to receive all the good things in life (vv. 4–12). Furthermore, all my own efforts to remain 'pure in heart' (v. 1) seem only to be rewarded by increased sufferings and mocking (vv. 13–15). Over half the Psalm is spent moaning and complaining about how doubtful this declared truth appears in my own experience of life.

But at verses 15–17, our perspective is anchored by drawing our attention to the fuller glory of God's goodness. Though God's goodness is not always visible in my present experience, nonetheless, his goodness remains certain. And it is in worship ('I went into the sanctuary of God;' v. 17) that I am enabled to experience that goodness of God in his promises, even if I do not yet see them worked out in my experience.

The remainder of the Psalm (vv. 18–28) helps me, with my heart now opened and the issues on the table, to ponder the certainty of God's promises to his people, and of divine judgment upon the wicked. This talk of judgment is not to tantilize us with some kind of cruel excitement over the destruction of the wicked who now prosper; rather, in understanding that God *is* a good judge, and that he will undo every wrong done to me (by judging the wicked) and will reward all holiness (despite my present suffering for it), my soul is nourished. If it does not all take place in the course of my experience now, God's good rewards are eternally certain for those who love him.

Indeed, by the end of the Psalm, we are led in words of praise to resolve (with Christ, our mediator): 'for me it is good to be near to God; I have made the Lord GOD my refuge.' (v. 28).

This kind of meditational singing is typical of the Psalms. Some Psalms are more complaining in their tone, others are more laudatory in their tone. But typically each of the Psalms involve some kind of declaration of truth about God, which is then pondered and exercised in a highly emotive manner designed to draw our own hearts and experiences into meditation, resulting then in a maturing of our faith in fidelity and praise.

Luther called the Psalms a 'little Bible' for this reason: because all the doctrines taught elsewhere in the Bible are, in the Psalms, recapitulated here in song.[47] Likewise Calvin famously described the Psalms as an 'anatomy of the human soul,' because all of man's emotions are engaged in the course of the Psalms meditations.[48]

What I am describing here is certainly no new discovery; but it involves a fundamentally different 'heart action' in our hymnody than the contemporary worship movement represents. It is thus a use of the Psalms that we need to conscientiously hang onto amidst contrary assumptions through today's church, where the expectation is that songs simply declare praise.

Psalmody as meditation: Deuteronomy 31–33

A great portion of Scripture that helps us think about the 'meditational' nature of biblical hymns is in the closing of

47   M. Luther, *Luther's Works*, 35.254 (see 39 n. 23, above).

48   Calvin, *Psalms*, xxxvii.

the book of Deuteronomy (ch. 31–33). There, as one of his final acts before the people head into the Promised Land, Moses composes two texts. Under divine instruction, Moses composed a book of law (31:24), and he also composed a song (31:22). Moses presented the lawbook, in writing, to the priests and elders; he taught the song, orally, to the congregation. It is the co-publication of these two texts which is significant for our attention. These two texts – the law and the song – have so close a relationship in the account as to be seemingly confused at times.

For example, both the book and the song are said to serve the same purpose for the people: they are both regarded as a 'witness' in their midst (vv. 19, 26). Furthermore, in 32:44–6, Moses recites 'all the words of this song' to the people, and then having done so, he exhorts the people to 'observe all the words of this law,' thereby identifying the song just sung to the people with the law given to their rulers.

One scholar who notes this tightly integrated relationship between the lawbook and song in this passage writes:

> The psalm…is taught to the whole people (31:19, 22, 30), whereas the law is transmitted to the Levites and elders (31:9, 25, 28). This difference in the material's intended transmission depicts the psalm as a popular synopsis of the law, which by its poetic form is better able to transmit Deuteronomic notions to a large audience than the law book itself can…The emphasis on [the song's] oral as well as written transmission presents the psalm as a popularly accessible summary of…[the lawbook's] theology and thus a counterpart to the law-book itself.[49]

Is this simply a feature of *this* song, on account of its contemporaneous publication with the Mosaic lawbook? Watts is prob-

---

49   J. Watts, *Psalm and Story,* p67.

ably correct when he concludes: 'The narrative role of Deuteronomy 32:1–43 provides evidence…of assumptions and expectations regarding psalmody in general.'[50] If this is correct, then Deuteronomy 31–33 is teaching us something important about the function of congregational hymnody: psalmody served as a means of 'law-meditation' – a means for popular contemplation on the theology taught in the companion lawbook.[51]

We might roughly think of the song as a workbook which accompanies its textbook, helping the student to exercise his (subjective) understanding of the truths which are taught (objectively) in the companion textbook.

It is, afterall, the song that will 'stick' in the people's memory, Moses explains (31:21). During ancient times, the importance of such a lawbook surrogate is evident. Written texts were not commonplace; the typical Hebrew believer could not log onto Amazon.com from the family homestead in the Judean hills to order a family Bible. Even if copies of the scrolls were to be mass-produced through some Hurculean, Levitical publishing program, the average Hebrew worshiper was illiterate. How could the average Hebrew remain nourished and anchored in the faith 'day and night' amidst the struggles and trials of life?

The lawbook was to be read publically in the worship festivals (Deut. 31:10–13). Furthermore, Levitical teachers were commissioned to instruct the people in the law amongst their various communities (2 Chron. 17:7–9). But apart from these gatherings, the people of ancient Israel had no means of access to the written word. It was the songs of worship that remained in the hearts of the congregants, and which continued to witness to them the lawbook's teachings 'day and night' (cf., Ps. 63:2, 6). The importance of such memorable

---

50   J. Watts, *Psalm and Story,* 80.

51   Cf., J. McConville, *Deuteronomy,* p461; P. Miller, *Deuteronomy,* 225–6.

surrogates, facilitating the people's meditation on the truths learned from the book, cannot be overstated.

I will, in this place, refrain from entering into a study of the song in Deuteronomy 32, itself (or its companion hymn in chapter 33). Such a study would allow us to identify themes of God's promises and his threatenings from the lawbook which are, indeed, summarized in the song. Even a cursory reading, furthermore, demonstrates that this is not a hymn which simply declares God's praiseworthiness (nor is it a hymn designed to make the people feel good about themselves). It is there to help the people cling, and even after spiritual decline to return, to fidelity and praise through contemplating God's law.

So, the lawbook of Moses was published with a companion hymn (and possibly hymnal).[52] The purpose of that hymn was to aid the congregation in meditation on the truths inscribed in the lawbook, resulting in praise and fidelity to God. Therefore, from the very beginning of Israel's national worship, Israel's hymns were for meditation leading to praise (not simple declaration of praise).

Let me carry this insight, now, back to the Davidically mediated praisebook: the Book of Psalms.

---

52 The fact that the unique name for Israel, *Jeshurun*, is central to this song (v. 15; cf., 33:26) invites speculation that this hymn might have been the 'title song' in the pre-Davidic, tabernacle-era hymnal, called the *Book of Jashar*, to which subsequent rulers appear to have added hymns (e.g., Josh. 10:13; 2 Sam. 1:8) up until the time of David's new temple organzation, including a new hymnal (the *Book of Psalms*). Perhaps the various, cultic changes involved in the move from tabernacle to temple worship under the Davidic covenant included a replacement of this old *Book of Jashar* with the *Psalms of David*. (Cf., D. Christensen, 'Jashar, Book of,' 3.646–7.); M. LeFebvre, 'The Hymns of Christ: The Old Testament Formation of the New Testament Hymnal'.

Hymnody as meditation: Psalm 1

We find confirmation of this principle as we note that the Psalter itself opens with an exhortation to meditate on God's law (Ps. 1). It is generally recognized that Psalm 1 serves as an introduction to the whole Book of Psalms.[53] Notably, it is a Psalm that exhorts us to meditate on God's law.

Psalm 1 tells a story. It is a story of a man who is happy – extremely joyful. Yet his circumstances cause us to wonder why. For he is described (in v. 1) as a happy man ('how blessed/ happy is the man'), but he is surrounded by sin and temptation ('the counsel of the wicked,' 'the way of sinners,' and 'the seat of scoffers.')

But the reason he is so happy, despite his trying circumstances, is because he possesses a grand hope. He sees that one day, the congregation of the righteous will stand in God's presence in community together (v. 5). Right now, he is a 'lonely outsider' in a society of sinners; but one day, he will be an 'insider' in the congregation of the righteous gathered in God's courts. At that time, it is the wicked man who, like chaff, will be cast out as the 'outsider' (v. 4). Psalm 1 is showing us the possibility of joy, now, in a broken world – and the way that this godly man attains to it. It is through his 'meditation on the law of the LORD day and night' (v. 2), and its nurturing promises of a great, eternal kingdom God is preparing.

What is this pious discipline which brings such great joy to the believer's heart? What is this exercise Psalm 1 describes as 'delighting in God's law' through 'meditating (Heb., *hagah*) on it day and night' (v. 2)? Commentators often think it strange that Israel's song book is introduced by the example of a man who is meditating on – presumably reading – God's lawbook.

---

53   See, M. Lefebvre, 'What is the Shape of the Psalter?' 4–5, 15.

But is this happy man *reading* the lawbook? Or is he *singing* about God's law?

Let me venture a little bit of Hebrew study with you. (I'll try to keep this painless!) The verb that is translated 'meditate' in verse 2 is the Hebrew word *hagah*. This verb simply means to 'vocalize' something, and does not in itself tell us whether the one '*hagah*-ing' is specifically reading, talking, moaning, or singing. We have to decide from the context which of these kinds of vocalization is taking place. But what the verb *hagah* does tell us is that the man is engaging with God's law in an audible voice – he is not meditating silently..

The English word 'meditate' is a good translation (for reasons I will note in a moment). But it carries the unfortunate connotation of something being done *silently*. The Hebrew verb is actually vocal, however.[54] In Proverbs 8:7, for example, *hagah* is used of Wisdom crying out in the streets. In Psalm 1, also, *hagah* refers to something done vocally (not silently).

Commentators who recognize the vocal nature of *hagah* generally draw one of the following three conclusions about the 'happy man' of Psalm 1: (1) he is reciting something memorized;[55] (2) he is reading something written;[56] or, (3) he is making inarticulate groans, sobs, and murmurs in the midst

54   A. Negoită and H. Ringgren, '*hāgāh*,' 3.321–24. M. Van Pelt and W. Kaiser, '*hgh* I,' 1.1006–8. Cf. N. Sarna, *On the Book of Psalms*, 38–39.

55   E.g., N. Sarna, *On the Book of Psalms*, 36; R. Davidson, *Vitality of Worship*, 11.

56   Even private reading in the ancient world was typically done vocally, not silently. On Ps. 1:2 as instruction to read the lawbook: e.g., N. Whybray, *Reading the Psalms*, 38–40. It has recently become common to speak of the Psalter itself as the 'law text' here promoted for reading (e.g., B. Childs, *Introduction to the Old Testament*, 513; J. Mays, 'The Place of Torah-Psalms in the Psalter,' 4–5; G. Wilson, *Application Commentary: Psalms*, 1.96.)

of deeply emotional thoughts.[57] A fourth possibility which is rarely mentioned, however, is that (4) he is singing.

This is surprising, since at least three out of ten uses of the same verb (*hagah*) in the Psalter itself explicitly have singing in view:[58]

> *…my mouth will praise you with joyful lips,*
> *when I remember you upon my bed,*
> *and* hagah *on you in the watches of the night…*
> *in the shadow of your wings I will sing for joy (63:5–7).*

> *I will also praise you with the harp…*
> *I will sing praises to you with the lyre, O Holy One of Israel.*
> *My lips will shout for joy,*
> *when I sing praises to you…*
> *And my tongue will* hagah *of your righteous help*
> *all the day long (71:22–4).*

> *I said, 'Let me remember my song in the night;*
> *let me meditate (Heb.,* siach*) in my heart.'*
> *Then my spirit made a diligent search…*
> *I said, 'I will…*hagah *[on] all your work,*
> *and meditate (Heb.,* siach*) on your mighty deeds (77:6–12).*

Others of the ten uses of this verb in the Psalms may also refer to singing, but these three are explicit.

The composer of Psalm 1 did not use a verb which requires that singing be understood (e.g. the Hebrew verb, *shir*, 'to sing'). The word *hagah* was used, not to require a certain kind

---

57 E.g., S. Terrien, *Psalms*, 73.

58 The ten uses of *hagah* in the Psalter: Pss 1:2; 2:1; 35:28; 37:30; 38:12; 63:6; 71:24; 77:12; 115:7; 143:5. Cf., also, the three appearances of the noun form, *higgaion* ('meditation'): 9:16; 19:14; 92:3.

of vocalization, but rather to focus our attention on the depth and quality of 'heart activity' going on behind that expression.

When the verb *hagah* is used in Hebrew, it is chosen in order to draw attention to the particular quality of a person's speech. The Hebrew linguist, Anastasie Negoiță, provides the following explanation:

> ...hāghāh is not a common word for speaking. Hebrew has other words for this, like 'āmar, dibber, or qāra'. On the other hand, hāghāh is sometimes used to express the feelings of the human soul. With śîach in particular, hāghāh means that a man 'is lost in his religion,' that he is filled with thoughts of God's deeds or his will.[59]

In other words, this verb is used instead of any other speech-verb when the writer wants to draw our attention to the deep, internal, wholehearted sentiments involved in that vocalization. This verb is like a transparency: it lends a certain coloring to the scene it overlays (the wholehearted character of the speech), but does not itself give shape to the action taking place (defining the kind of speech occuring). This is why the translation 'meditate' is so commonly used in Psalm 1, and rightly so. But we make a mistake if we assume that this meditation is being accomplished through reading or recitation, specifically. It could be accomplished in many ways, including singing.

In fact, since this Psalm extols the value of such deep and thoughtful meditation at the beginning of a collection of *sung* meditations, singing should be seen as the most prominent of the many kinds of meditation Psalm 1 is encouraging. The law of the Lord describes the righteous community which God has

---

59   A. Negoiță and H. Ringgren, '*hagah*,' 323. Cf., J. McCann, *NIB: Psalms*, 4.960: 'The verb describes the orientation of one's whole existence.'

promised to form from his people, and for the lonely man of Psalm 1 dwelling in the city of wickedness, singing the songs that ponder what God's law teaches is a source of great delight.[60]

One reason I belabor this point is because, if you pick up commentaries on the Psalms, you will encounter a general trend toward the opposite assumption among scholars today. Many scholars follow Brevard Childs's suggestion in his 1979 book, *Introduction to the Old Testament as Scripture*. Childs there proposed that the man in Psalm 1 is *reading* a book, and that the purpose of Psalm 1 is to change this collection of hymns into texts for reading rather than singing.[61] As one scholar states, speaking of Psalm 1:

> Its introductory position alters the function of the Psalter for postexilic ancient Israel. The psalms that had once been used as cultic songs *to* YHWH are now to be listened to as instruction *from* YHWH.[62]

This is an amazing conclusion to draw when the main verb in Psalm 1 actually says nothing at all about *the kind* of speech being employed (e.g., reading versus singing), but simply its wholehearted character! Furthermore, as we noted in chapter 1 of this book, it was only in recent centuries that the church actually did begin to emphasize reading the Psalms over singing them. The evidence of 'postexilic ancient Israel' and beyond is actually quite strong that the Psalms continued to

60   On the nature of the Psalms as sung meditations on God's law, see: P. Miller, 'Deuteronomy and Psalms.'

61   B. Childs, *Introduction to the Old Testament*, p513: 'Psa. 1 has assumed a highly significant function as a preface to the psalms which are to be read, studied, and meditated upon.'

62   N. DeClaisse-Walford, *Reading from the Beginning*, p43. Cf., G. Wilson, *Application Commentary: Psalms*, 1.92 (n9), 96; C. Broyles, *NIBC: Psalms*, 5; McCann, 'The Psalms as Instruction'; *NIB: Psalms*, 4.642, 665–6; Klaus Seybold, *Introducing the Psalms*, 24; Mays, *Psalms*, 15–16, 40–44.

be sung to God. Psalm 1 can hardly have introduced such a radical transformation of the use of the Psalms as many scholars nowadays suppose.

While singing is certainly not the only way to meditate on Scripture,[63] it was an important means employed in ancient Israel. Singing is the primary means of meditation Psalm 1 has in view, since it is a book of songs that this Psalm introduces. Psalm 1 employs the verb *hagah* simply as an encouragement to use these meditations on God's law wholeheartedly, in order to experience the joy in our hearts that such sung-meditations are designed to bring about. Psalm 1 is urging that 'heart activity,' as we sing, which will give us delight and praise in the midst of a sinful world.[64]

The same lawbook/songbook principle taught at the end of the Bible's five-volume lawbook is repeated at the beginning of its five-volume hymnbook.

Hymnody as meditation: Colossians 3:16

Thus far, we have looked at psalmody as 'meditation' from two Old Testament texts: one at the close of the biblical lawbook; the other at the opening of the biblical hymnbook. The Apostle Paul represents this same 'heart activity' for the

---

63   Cf., Josh. 1:8, where Joshua is specifically charged to meditate on '*the book* of the law' (i.e., by reading, since *the book* of the law is specified; in Ps. 1:2, however, no book is mentioned, further leaning our interpretation toward other forms of law meditation here, not exclusively reading).

64   This interpretation of Psalm 1's introductory emphasis on *delight* is contrary to the view of Walter Brueggeman's influential article suggesting that Psalm 1 emphasized *obedience*. (W. Brueggeman, 'Bounded by Obedience and Praise.') He assumes that the reason for meditating on God's law is to foster obedience. However, Psalm 1 actually says nothing about obedience; rather, it tells us that the fruit of meditation on God's law here in view is delight. (Cf., G. Grogan, *Psalms,* 262.)

New Testament church's singing, as well. In his letter to the Colossians, Paul gave this familiar exhortation on singing:

> Let the word of Christ dwell in you richly in all wisdom, teaching and admonishing one another in psalms and hymns and spiritual songs, singing with grace in your hearts to the Lord (Col. 3:16, NKJV).

We have already noted, in the previous chapter, the conversational setting of the church's singing described here: God, the congregation, and Christ are all involved in this 'singing conversation.' In this chapter, I want to point out the meditational nature of the church's part in this 'sung conversation'.

Paul here describes church singing as an activity whereby the word of Christ produces wisdom, and that richly, in our hearts. Not only are we *personally* meditating on the king's word through his songs, but we are *corporately* meditating ('teaching and admonishing one another'). Finally, it is a process which produces 'grace in the heart' to the Lord. This grace in the heart is a product of the sung-meditation, and this grace is our praise to the Lord.

According to this description of praise by Paul, it is not the Psalms' words themselves that are the fullness of our praise to God. What praises God is when our sung-meditations, in the word of Christ, stir graces in our hearts to the Lord. In other words, even if we sing great hymns in our worship, we do not produce the full praise God desires unless we are singing them meditatively to stir up the inner depths of our hearts. That is what the Psalms are designed to do.

This is not, however, what we are used to doing when we sing in the church today. We have come to expect smooth and beautiful descriptions of God's ways in our songs. But the Psalms are messy, complex wrestling matches between God's ways and worldly temptations. It feels odd to the modern congregation to have so much of worldly temptation and confusion included in our hymnody. It is no wonder, therefore, Isaac Watts and the English hymnwriting movement found the biblical Psalms unsatisfactory for Christian worship (as we noted in chapter one). But it is not gracious words that praise God; it is grace in the heart produced by sung-meditation that praises God. This is a speciality of the Psalms.

My kids love going to the drive thru car wash with me. They have great fun watching all the soapers and wipers scrubbing the car as we go through. I tend to think of Psalm singing as a bit like pulling up to a drive thru car wash. You come up to the Psalm with all the natural dirt and disappointment of life, and the Psalm meets you there. But you pull your wheels onto the tracks, and then let the Psalm lead your thought process from there. Follow the Psalm, as it carries you through sprayers, scrubbers, heat, and the perfectly tailored process of meditation designed to sanctify and hearten your faith.

This means paying attention when we sing (not just letting the music put us into a trance). But the rewards of such meditational Psalm singing are as glorious as the visions of praise and heaven held out to us in its songs.

Now we see why the Psalms are so awkward for modern churches. They are designed for a different kind of 'heart motion' than churches in the bent of the English hymnwriting movement are used to. We pick up screws and expect to pound them; we pick up Psalms and expect to praise with them (rather than stirring praise with them). So they feel awkward. But the problem is not with the Psalms, but with our changed expectations of what a hymn is supposed to accomplish.

To make the most fruitful use of the Psalms which Christ has given us, we have to recover a meditational approach to singing.

Martin Luther once asked, 'What is the whole Psalter but meditation and exercises based on the First Commandment?' Luther's statement underscores a special relationship between the Psalms and the First Commandment. The First Commandment is to serve God exclusively and faithfully: 'You shall have no other gods before me' (Exod. 20:3). It is that standard of faithfulness which Psalm singing helps sustain in the face of worldly trials and temptations. As 'meditation and exercises,' Psalm singing is a means of God's grace for Christian faith.

But to sing the Psalms as 'meditation[s] and exercises,' we must sing them thoughtfully. The Apostle Paul emphasized the importance of thoughtful singing when he wrote, 'I will sing praise with my spirit, but I will sing with my mind also' (1 Cor. 14:15; cf., John 8:32).

When you sing Psalms, pay attention to them. If it helps, sing slowly in order to focus on the words and not just the tune. It might help to read a Psalm before you sing it. Consult a commentary once in awhile to explore the message of a Psalm before you make it your own confession of faith by singing it.

In a congregational setting, it is important to help worshipers develop the discipline of singing with understanding. Some churches pick one Psalm each Lord's Day to be 'the Psalm of the Week,' and give a ten-minute explanation before singing it. A Psalm explanation should draw attention to the truths we are wrestling with and confessing as we sing that Psalm. Starting with Psalm 1 and moving sequentially through the Psalm book, one Psalm a week, a church can sing through the entire Psalter in three years. Through this practice, a congregation develops an ability to sing the Psalms with understanding.

6

Confusion and Glory (part 2):
Cursing in Faith
with the Psalms of Imprecation

Everyone was feeling edgy in Darius's capital. Alexander the Great had been marching from the western border of the empire, steadily advancing toward the heart of Persia. He had crushed every force that dared to oppose him. Darius called a counsel of war to plan an attack at Issus to stop the Macedonian advance.

According to the ancient Greek historian, Diodorus, one of the advisors to King Darius at that conference was a mercenary named Charidemus. Things got so tense during the deliberations that Charidemus lost his cool and accused the king of cowardice. In an outburst of rage at this insult, Darius commanded that Charidemus be taken away and executed. The guards hastened Charidemus to 'death row,' where he was held while preparations for his execution were made.

It was not long before, according to Diodorus, 'the king's passion had cooled,' and he regretted his verdict against

Charidemus. Darius labored to reverse the charges and free Charidemus before it was too late. However, even the king, according to Persian law, could not undo a verdict once imposed. Charidemus was executed, with the king standing by full of regret.[65] (Oh, and by the way, the battle at Issus also went badly for Darius.)

Can you identify with Darius's regrettable loss of temper? All through the ages, even kings are known to lose their cool and say things they later regret. What about the angry outbursts of the king who sings in the Psalms?

There are places in the Psalms where the anger behind the words is unmistakable. And in those heated stanzas, some Psalms even break into curses against foes. Was King David 'just losing his cool' like King Darius the Persian?

Consider the shocking imprecation of Psalm 109:

May his days be few;
may another take his office!
May his children be fatherless
and his wife a widow…
May there be none to extend kindness to him…
May his posterity be cut off…

As noted in chapter one of this book, it was because of lines like these that leaders of the modern hymn writing movement sought to replace Psalm singing with new songs. Believing such expressions were regretable – even 'un-Christian' – they wrote new hymns. But before we jump to the conclusion that our praises should be empty of such harsh words, maybe we should consider why these curses were part of Israel's praises in the first place. Is it regretable that such imprecations are

---

65   Diodorus, *Histories*, 17.30.1–7. (Cf., the similar account of Daniel's condemnation, with a much happier outcome, in Dan. 6:1–29.)

here; or, are the condemnations in the Psalms an important part of Christian praise that we are missing in contemporary worship?

The imprecation just quoted from Psalm 109 was specifically identified by Peter as being words of Jesus (and became the basis for replacing Judas) in Acts 1:20. Yes, these kinds of prayers are uncomfortable (they are supposed to be!), but they are there, given by God and led by Christ, for us to sing. Curses in the Psalms are not provided for us to sing with relish, but even these hard lines are there for our faith and worship.

Just to be clear: imprecatory Psalms are relatively rare within the Psalter. It is out of proportion with the Psalter's own dimensions to devote an entire chapter to them in this book. Nonetheless, the challenge which these harsh Psalms pose for those who want to sing the Psalms, and to do so in Christian grace, is important enough to deserve attention. In this chapter, I want to look at the role of the imprecatory Psalms in Christian faith and worship.

The place of judgment in the Christian faith

The first thing we need to do is clarify the role of judgment, in general, in the Christian faith. Perhaps a good place to start is with the paradigmatic display of divine judgment given early in Genesis: the flood. Everyone knows the story of Noah, his ark, and all the animals he carried with him to safety during the flood. But have you ever noticed what the meaning of Noah's name is, and the way in which his story is introduced?

In the closing verses of Genesis 5, Noah's story is introduced with a prophecy from his father. It is this prophecy of Noah's father which explains the flood that came in Noah's day:

> When Lamech had lived 182 years, he fathered a son and called his name Noah (Heb., *nōach*), saying, 'Out of the ground that

the Lord has cursed this one shall bring us relief (Heb., *nācham*; lit., 'rest') from our work and from the painful toil of our hands' (Gen. 5:28–9).

Noah's father, Lamech, was among that line of believers who continued to look for the One, promised to Adam, who would deliver them from the curse pronounced in Eden. Noah was not to be the Messiah, himself; but he was to be one, serving in the redemptive work of Christ, bringing *rest* to God's people. This is why Lamech named his son 'Noah,' meaning 'rest.'

Isn't that interesting? The name of Noah, and the work God was to perform in his day, was to be a work of rest. It would be a great judgment – a dreadful judgment, purging the world of that day of all kinds of evildoers. But the purpose of that judgment was rest.

When politicians in America seek an executive office – whether mayor, governor, or president – one of the promises they often make is that they will be 'tough on crime.' We know that, when wickedness reigns unchecked on our streets, the city is unsafe and all that is good comes to a standstill. But it is the mark of a governor's love for all that is right, and of a courtroom magistrate's goodness, when evildoers are given urgent exhortations to abandon their ways, and are stopped if they persist.

In such a manner, God appointed Noah to preach to his generation for 120 years. Although he does not seem to have had much fruit from his preaching, he seems to have found godly spouses for his three sons. Nonetheless, when the time came, God delivered Noah and his family, but poured down a terrible judgment upon the wicked.

When the judge's gavel drops and justice is executed, only then do the righteous receive relief from the violence and moral wrongs of their afflictors. In times of especially intense affliction, it is the hope that such judgment will come that provides comfort and strength to the suffering soul. Indeed, everyone who looks forward to the return of Christ and the close of the ages, is hoping for the rest that only comes when judgment is executed. The expectation of judgment is an inseparable feature of Christian hope.

Indeed, while it has sometimes been argued that the imprecations in the Psalms are remnants of an 'Old Testament ethic' which has no place in the Christian church, we have to recognize that prayers for judgment are as much a feature of the New Testament church as the Old.

In Mark 11:12–26, the Evangelist reports an imprecation that Jesus announced against the temple. In Matthew 23:1–36, Jesus delivers a series of curses against the scribes and pharisees. On the Isle of Cyprus, Paul called down judgment upon Elymas (Acts 13:10–11). Peter likewise pronounced Christ's judgment on Simon the magician in Acts 8:20. In fact, in Galatians 1:8–9, Paul actually instructs us to pronounce Christ's curse on those who bring heresy into the church (cf., Titus 3:10–11; 1 John 5:16). Furthermore, in the Book of Revelation, we are told that the saints in heaven pray for judgment on the foes of the church (Rev. 6:10).

Imprecation is not strictly an Old Testament feature. It is found all through the Scriptures, even on the lips of the apostles, of Christ himself, and in the assemblies in heaven.[66] But in all these examples, the judgments announced are articulations of God's judgment, not personal vendetta. That is crucial to recognize. Furthermore, it is significant to recognize that Jesus' aforementioned curses in Mark 11 and Matthew 23,

66   John N. Day produced an excellent dissertation while studying at Dallas Theological Seminary on 'The Imprecatory Psalms and Christian Ethics' that explores the relationship between Old and New Testament curses. His work has recently been published under the title, *Crying for Justice,* and has been summarized in an article in *Bibliotheca Sacra,* 'The Imprecatory Psalms and Christian Ethics.'

are both immediately followed by teaching on forgiveness (Mark 11:24–5) and restoration (Matt. 23:37–39).

It is not that Jesus is 'regreting' his imprecations in these further lines about forgiveness. Rather, he is showing us that judgment is not out of harmony with the gospel of grace and forgiveness. Furthermore, he is teaching us that we must have a heart of grace, even when we do announce God's judgment.

A passage from the Apostle might be helpful at this point. In Romans 12, Paul teaches the church to 'bless those who persecute you; bless and curse not.' He tells us that the basis upon which we can let go of offenses against us is because we know that God will exact his judgments on these offenses: 'leave it to the wrath of God,' Paul continues, 'for it is written, "Vengeance is mine, I will repay"' (Rom. 12:14–21). According to Paul, the reason we do not curse offenders *with our own curses,* is because we expect *God's curses* to be brought to bear on the wicked.

Here, then, is an important distinction we find in the biblical teaching on judgment. In all moral and physical wrongs, the Christian is to acknowledge that God is the Judge (not me). Therefore, we refrain from presuming to choose and inflict our own judgments on those who wrong us. Nevertheless, just as we readily announce the promise of God's forgiveness on all who repent, so we also announce the promise of *God's* judgment on all who do not repent. This is part of the gospel proclamation, and there are Psalms to help us sing of God's judgment (that brings rest) in a messy world, just as there are Psalms to help us sing of his forgiveness (that brings restoration).

Singing imprecation – Psalm 137

Of the various imprecatory lines in the Psalter, probably none has caused as much difficulty as the vivid expressions in Psalm 137. This is the Psalm which closes with the graphic words of judgment against Edom and Babylon (v. 9):

> *Blessed shall he be who takes your little ones*
> *and dashes them against the rock!*

Reading commentaries on this Psalm, you will find all manner of ways in which men try to explain this awful description. Some commentators attempt to explain it away as a feature of Old Testament morality, not suited for New Testament faith.[67] Others believe that the psalmist is venting hatred in these lines which is sinful, and simply should be called 'sinful.'[68] Others soften the image by turning it into a metaphor for cutting off 'the infantile beginnings of small indulgences [to sin],'[69] thus sidestepping the fact that the Psalm is actually talking about real infants. Perhaps the most striking approach is to simply delete verse 9, as many liturgical and metrical settings of the Psalms have done.[70]

All these approaches are demonstrations of a spirit of Christian grace seeking to make sense of how so horrible a petition should fit into Christian hymnody. But rather than sidestepping or softening the image (it is supposed to be dreadful; judgment is a terrible thing), we'll best appreciate its place in the Christian faith by making sense of its role within this Psalm.

Let me walk you through Psalm 137, as we think about how to fruitfully sing an imprecation like this as followers of Christ.

67   E.g., R. Zuck, 'Problem of the Imprecatory Psalms,' 73.

68   E.g., W. Brueggemann, *Message of the Psalms*, 85–6; P. Craige, *WBC: Psalms 1–50*, 1.50.

69   C. Lewis, *Reflections on the Psalms*, 136.

70   E.g., in J. Bell, *Psalms of Patience, Protest and Praise*. Note that Bell does state, in this songbook, that the last verse of Psa 137 should be included when preaching this Psalm, even if omitted when singing it.

The opening verses (vv. 1–4) give us the tone and setting of this sad hymn:

> *By the waters of Babylon,*
> *there we sat down and wept,*
> *when we remembered Zion.*
> *On the willows there we hung up our lyres.*
> *For there our captors required of us songs,*
> *and our tormentors, mirth, saying,*
> *'Sing us one of the songs of Zion!'*
> *How shall we sing the LORD's song*
> *in a foreign land?*

Historically, the Psalm is recalling the exile of Judah into Babylon (2 Kings 24–25). Around 587 BC, Nebuchadnezzar's army had fallen upon Jerusalem. Raping, pillaging, burning, plundering, and torturing the Jews, the Babylonian army devestated the kingdom, carrying off the survivors into captivity.

I never really appreciated how utterly devestating a war like that would have been until I visited the British Museum in London and spent several hours studying the carved stone images from Sennacharib's seige of Lachish (cf., 2 Chron. 32:9). If you ever get the opportunity to go to the British Museum, let me encourage you to study closely the 62 feet of engraved tablets that retell that story with dramatic images of period warfare. It is a presentation just as gripping as any Stephen Spielberg war movie, though accomplished simply in the media of stone. The victors in such a siege would have been brutal.

I think one of the reasons Christians in the modern West tend not to know what to do with imprecatory Psalms like this is because we rarely experience the kinds of settings they are designed for. Maybe we should not sing these cursing Psalms often, but we must remember that the Psalter is not designed for use by Christians living lives of ease and security, alone.

It is designed for the church's use across all ages and cultures, and in all kinds of circumstances. And there are times when the persecution and cruelty against God's people reaches such a fervor that we need Christ-led hymns of justice like this to guide us in what to do with all the deep pain and turmoil we experience. Indeed, even in the comfortable life of the West, there are circumstances of abuse and deep emotional and spiritual turmoil that need Christ-led songs of justice and 'closure' as part of his gospel's redemptive work. The days after the Babylonian conquest were clearly such a time.

Anguish is running high in this Psalm. But notice in these opening lines, that the Babylonian cruelty *against us* is not the main focus here. What grieves us most deeply of all is how they have mocked the Lord and defiled *his* house in their cruelties to this people! This is not a song of personal vengeance; it is a song which helps us to 'remember Zion' in this time of sorrow, and how the torment of these foes is ultimately torment of God's family. Recall how, on the road to Damascus, Christ appeared to Saul the persecutor and said to him, 'Saul, Saul, why are you persecuting *me*?' (Acts 9:4). In our love for the Lord, it is the offense against him in such violence against his children that this Psalm brings to the center of our song (cf., Matt. 18:6).

First of all, in Psalm 137, we remember what they did to violate God's house in the past ('we remember Zion'). Furthermore, then, we agonize that the mocking and persecution continues and will not stop. Even here, back in Babylon, 'our captors required of us songs…saying, "Sing us one of the songs of Zion!" How shall we sing the LORD's song in a foreign land?'

The point here is that the Babylonians were continuing to mock Israel's God. They were asking the captives to sing the songs which boast of God's greatness, all the while laughing in mirth at the God whom these Hebrew Psalms celebrate with such majesty, but whose house and people *they* had just humbled. The response of the captives was to hang their harps and weep: how could they sing of the glory and majesty of God who had just let this happen?

Isn't that a feeling which you have at least encountered, in some form or another, before? How can I praise a God who just let *this* happen (whatever, in your experience, the 'this' might be)? And that is where a Psalm like 137 is vital for sustaining Christian faith and praise. When we have sinned, we need to turn to Psalms of repentance. When God has been mocked, we need hymns that help us to wrestle with that, too. Notice how verses 5–6 lead us to cling to our faith:

> *If I forget you, O Jerusalem,*
> *let my right hand forget its skill!*
> *Let my tongue stick to the roof of my mouth,*
> *if I do not remember you,*
> *if I do not set Jerusalem*
> *above my highest joy!*

Because of the shocking image of the condemnation called down on the children of Babylon and Edom in verse 9, we often overlook the fact that the imprecation of this Psalm is actually double-sided. And the first imprecation is invoked against myself, when I sing it.

How can I praise God in the midst of the utter collapse of the church before the world? The sense to which verses 1–5 brings us is one of surrender: we cannot sing any longer. But we must. And that is the determined resolve which now emerges. I must continue to play my harp; I must continue to sing to the God of Jerusalem with my tongue. In fact, if during these years of captivity and oppression, we set aside the Psalms of faith and glory and abandon our faith in God's sovereign redemption, may it be that my hand and my tongue serve no other purpose. The very purpose for which I exist is to glorify God, and if that stops, then so must everything else I do.

God did bring his people out of the captivity in Babylon, although it was seventy years before the first wave of remnants returned (Jer. 29:10; Ezra 1:1). By then, many had become so integrated into the places where they now lived (Babylon would have been the only home that the new generation of Hebrews knew) returning to rebuild devestated homeland was not attractive any longer. Ezra had a tough time recruiting enough people to go back with him (Ezra 8:15-20). But, in God's providence, there were those who still 'remembered Jerusalem above their highest joy' while living in captivity, and devoted themselves to the work.

In a wedding ceremony, a couple stands before witnesses and takes vows to remain true to one another 'in sickness and in health, in plenty and in want, in joy and in sorrow.' How much more secure is the love of God, wherein we, in placing our faith in his covenant, pledge our devotion to him. In Psalm 137, Christ as our covenant king is leading us in a profession of faithfulness to God even in the deepest of sorrows and injustices. The first imprecation of this Psalm is one that we take upon ourselves.

Only secondly, then, do we find the Psalm leading us in pronouncing God's judgment upon the Babylonian and Edomite persecutors (vv. 7–9):

> Remember, O LORD, against the Edomites
> the day of Jerusalem,
> how they said, 'Lay it bare, lay it bare.
> down to its foundations!'
> O daughter of Babylon, doomed to be destroyed,
> blessed shall he be who repays you
> with what you have done to us!
> Blessed shall he be who takes your little ones
> and dashes them against the rock!

One of my favorite lines in C. S. Lewis's *Chronicles of Narnia* occurs when Mr and Mrs Beaver first tell Lucy about the lion Aslan (the Christ-figure in that allegory). Quite alarmed at this talk of a lion, Lucy asks, 'Is he quite safe?' to which Mr Beaver replies, 'Course he isn't safe. But he's good.' And so the thematic phrase is repeated throughout the story, 'He is not a tame lion.'[71]

Imprecatory Psalms remind us that Jesus is a good king, but not a 'tame' king. He is a just king, who loves his people and comes to their aid. Sometimes he brings peace to his church by bringing our persecutors to their knees in repentance and faith, like Saul who once ravaged the church but was converted himself into a great minister in the church (Acts 9:1–31). What a glorious deliverance that is when that happens! But sometimes God brings peace by exacting justice on persecutors, like when he brought Herod's sentence of death on James, and attempt to kill Peter, upon his own head, by which judgment 'the word of God increased and multiplied' (Acts 12:1–24).

In his own wisdom, God is the one who does these things, and we are not in a position to insist on one way or the other. And there are actually Scriptures that teach us both to pray for the forgiveness, and to pray for God's judgment, in the face of persecution. Is that a contradiction?

I find it interesting that the New Testament martyr, Stephen, was actually arrested because he was announcing imprecations against the apostate temple (Acts 6:14), and in his speech at his trial he directly condemned those who were persecuting him (vv. 51–53). Nevertheless, at the same time, he lifted his eyes toward heaven and prayed for God's forgiveness on his foes (v. 60). Subsequent events showed that both Stephen's expectations were right: God did bring judgment upon

---

71   C. S. Lewis, *Chronicles of Narnia*, p. 146 ('not a tame lion': e.g., 194, 677, 679, 682, 707).

the temple and its leadership (the temple was destroyed by the Romans in 70 AD), and he also brought repentance and forgiveness to at least one from amongst them (Saul) prior to that judgment. God brought rest to his church through both forgiveness and judgment, and Stephen was right to pray for both.

I recall again how Jesus, in his own teachings on imprecation, exhorted us to pray for judgment, but to do so with hearts of forgiveness. Let me quote Jesus' words on the matter, from the Gospel according to Mark. In the preceding paragraphs, Jesus had just announced a curse on the temple (through the figure of a fig tree) for failing to produce fruit for him. The disciples are amazed at the power of Jesus' word of judgment, which leads to this exchange between them:

> And Peter remembered and said to him, 'Rabbi, look! The fig tree that you cursed has withered.' And Jesus answered them, 'Have faith in God. Truly, I say to you, whoever says to this mountain [i.e., the temple mount], 'Be taken up and thrown into the sea,' and does not doubt in his heart, but believes that what he says will come to pass, it will be done for him. Therefore I tell you, whatever you ask in prayer, believe that you have received it, and it will be yours. And whenever you stand praying, forgive, if you have anything against anyone, so that your Father also who is in heaven may forgive you your trespasses' (Mark 11:21–26).

This passage from Jesus' ministry is often quoted as the basis for praying for whatever we want, in 'prosperity gospel' teaching. However, in its context it is actually teaching about imprecatory prayer. Jesus is teaching his disciples that they, also, will see such violations of God's name and his people that will lead them to pray for judgment as Jesus brought judgment 'on this mountain' before the eyes of the disciples. But Jesus was quick to add that, 'whenever you stand praying,' clear your own heart of bitterness and forgive. When God does come in judgment, you need to insure your heart is right so that you, yourself, do not fall under that judgment too.

Similarly, in Matthew 23, Jesus called down 'woes' upon the scribes and pharisees (vv. 1–33) and proclaimed judgment against Jerusalem '...so that on you may come [justice for] all the righteous blood shed on earth, from the blood of innocent Abel to the blood of Zechariah the son of Barachiah, whom you murdered between the sanctuary and the altar. Truly, I say to you, all these things will come upon this generation' (Matt. 23:34–6). Then, immediately after pronouncing that imprecation, he wept over the city with a heart to gather the people to himself:

> O Jerusalem, Jerusalem, the city that kills the prophets and stones those whom are sent to it! How often would I have gathered your children together as a hen gathers her brood under her wings, and you would not (Matt. 23:37).

There is, at the heart of the Christian faith, a gospel that announces both life and death, forgiveness and judgment, eternal life and eternal damnation. These are not contradictory, but rather express the unified glory of God applied to sinful humanity, saving many to life and passing over many to judgment. Jesus teaches us to pray according to the *fullness* of the gospel. And in the Psalms, he provides for our meditation and singing according to the fullness of the gospel.

In Psalm 137, after fixing our hearts on God's glory (and not personal vendetta), and after invoking imprecations on ourselves if we ourselves are unfaithful to him, Psalm 137:7–9 invokes God's judgment on the Babylonians and Edomites who had devestated the congregation of God's people.

It is crucial to note that it is *God's* judgment that is here proclaimed. The Psalm is not leading us to invent our own judgment, our own sense of 'what those Babylonians deserve,' and then attaching God's name to it. We have no right, either in blessing or in cursing, to announce our own ideas and then attatch God's name to it. The curses announced in Psalm 137 are a sung articulation of the judgments which the Lord himself had pronounced. The word of the Lord came to Isaiah during the exile, saying,

> The oracle concerning Babylon…I myself have commanded my consecrated ones, and have summoned my mighty men to execute my anger…Whoever is found will be thrust through, and whoever is caught will fall by the sword. Their infants will be dashed in pieces before their eyes (Isa. 13:1–16).

The similarity of wording between Isaiah 13 and Psalm 137 suggest that the Psalm is, indeed, invoking this known announcement of judgment already declared by God. It is not inventing a new judgment. It is a horrible warning that God had given! It is supposed to be horrible. None of us, especially parents of little ones, can or should enjoy that vision. But perhaps it is in Psalms like this that we finally come to realize just how horrible and treacherous human sin is before God. It is *that* horrible to God, that this indeed is just judgment. To quote the Scottish theologian William Binnie,

> Certainly, they [the imprecatory Psalms] ought never to be sung but with fear and trembling. Nevertheless, at fit seasons, they may and ought to find a place in our service of praise. It has been justly said that 'in a deep sense of moral evil, more perhaps than in anything else, abides a saving knowledge of God.'…As powerful witnesses for the truth that sin is hateful to God and deserving of His wrath and everlasting curse, – a truth which the world would

fain forget, – the Imprecatory Psalms must be accounted worthy of their place in the divine Manual of Praise.[72]

Without neutralizing the terror of the judgment described in this Psalm, its broader meaning ought to be understood. Such a command to destroy a nation, down to the littlest ones among them, is an instruction found in other war narratives, also (e.g., 1 Sam. 15:1–3; Nahum 3:7–10; Hosea 13:16; Jer. 6:11; 9:21). Although skeptics often point to these texts to suggest that the Christian faith endorses genocide, it must be firmly demonstrated that nowhere in Scripture is judgment ever brought on the basis of ethnicity. Judgments are always on the basis of sin, and a favorite theme of all such judgment narratives in Scripture is the repeated examples of members of the judged society coming out, repenting, and being saved prior to that judgment (e.g., Lot out of Sodom in Gen. 19; some Egyptians in the plagues and exodus in Exod. 9:20, 12:38; Rahab out of Jericho in Josh. 2; and so on). These scenes are not endorsements for genocide.[73] Indeed, the same kind of judgment, cutting off the entire family, is pronounced against those *within* the household of Israel as often as against those without! (E.g., the High Priest Eli, in 2 Sam. 2:30–34; Achan in Josh. 7:24; and others in Pss. 9:6; 34:16; 37:10; 41:5; 109:13–15) These announcements are not comparable to genocide. But they are there, and they do need to be understood.

There is a reason why the judgment of a people, down to the littlest among them (as took place in Noah's flood), is presented in Scripture as a cause of particular rest ('blessedness' in Psalm 137's terms). The 'blessing' of such a judgment is its *finality.*

72   W. Binnie, *Pathway into the Psalter,* 289.

73   Cf., chapter 4 ('The Church is Responsible for So Much Injustice') in: T. Keller, *The Reason for God.*

Babylon was a vicious foe of righteousness and peace ever since Nimrod rallied the masses to help construct the Tower of Babel on the site that became Babylon (Gen. 10:8–10; 11:1–9). In God's patience, thousands of years had been given for Babylon to repent. In God's dealing with rebellious peoples like this in the Old Testament, we often see one generation humbled only to find the next rising up again to renew the persecution against God's purposes.

The announcement of judgment down to the littlest is presented as a message of hope and rest, not because there is delight in such destruction (cf., Ezek. 18:32), but because of what it accomplishes. It is a *final* judgment, so that this persistent and perpetual source of persecution will now stop and be no more, forever. Violence will be laid to rest forever, never to rise again. It is always the announcement, not of judgment, but of *final* judgment, which brings true rest to God's people (cf., Ps. 34:16; 109:13–15).

God is patient. He tarries long that there might be time for many from amongst Babylon's spiritual heirs to come to repentance. In those years of tarrying, we must guard our hearts and hold fast to our faith in God's goodness, never letting the delay of his judgment lead us to cease singing his praises. But it is the great hope of the gospel that, one day, the angel of the Lord will indeed cry out the declaration of final rest: 'Fallen, fallen is Babylon!' (Rev 18:2) Never to rise again.

I was participating in a seminar on the Psalms in Glasgow, Scotland, some years ago. The subject of the imprecatory Psalms was the focus of one session, with contributing scholars from several different nations taking part.

One of the participants was a young priest from the Anglican Church in Rwanda. He spoke about the genocide in Rwanda in 1994, and how most of his own family was brutally slain in that violence. Three of his brothers were killed on the same day. It was painful for this man even to talk about those events. Then he told about the hundreds of missionaries who flooded into the nation after the violence had ceased – missionaries from the West who came instructing the people that they needed to forgive and reconcile with their brutal adversaries.

My colleague said that, while he and his fellow Christian survivors in Rwanda recognized the need for forgiveness, the messages from these missionaries seemed hollow. They simply did not understand the brutality of what they had experienced. But then he found Psalm 137 in his Bible. And he said to us, that in reading this Psalm, he found peace to trust God to bring justice and thereby to let go of the bitterness in his own heart. For in Psalm 137, he found that the psalm singer understands the necessity of justice to put things right again. And, ironically, he was able to forgive, because of Psalm 137.

After this young minister from Rwanda spoke, another young minister from Nigeria spoke. He described the unrest and bloodshed which his country has continually experiencd over the years. And he spoke about the comfort which believers in that land found in looking to God to bring judgment on the wicked. 'We need such Psalms,' he concluded.

Then, a minister from Pakistan spoke. He observed that, any time Christians today pray for their government leaders and their militaries to have wisdom and success in the modern 'war on terror,' those Christians *are* praying imprecatory prayers. Whether we realize it or not, such prayers are calling on God to bring the same kind of justice as the cursing Psalms invoke.

Men like these live and serve Jesus in circumstances we, in the West, have not experienced for a long time. Maybe the reason the modern hymnwriting movement sought to get away from such Psalms is because the relative peace of the West has brought us into circumstances where we don't perceive a need of them. But their presence reminds us that the Psalter is not just a hymnal for the affluent churches of the modern West. It is the hymnal for all God's church, in all times and places. And

Psalms like this help us to remember and to pray with, our persecuted brothers around the world in their afflictions.

The Psalms of imprecation are rare within the Psalter. And they are to be used humbly in Christ (not for personal angst). But because the gospel is a promise of redemption fulfilled through patient grace anticipating final judgment, these hymns too are an important part of Christian worship.

We should not be over eager to sing imprecatory Psalms. And we certainly should not use them with our own, personal grudges in mind. John Calvin reports that, in his day, a person could hire monks to sing imprecatory Psalms for days on end against a personal enemy. Use of these songs to bear personal animosities is sinful. But to ignore them altogether is also not right. Christ has given them to us as part of the chorus of spiritual rest we sing about in the Psalms.

When we sing these Psalms, we must sing them with a right heart: one of repentance for our own sins and longing for the repentance of others. But recognizing that there will be those who are so entrenched in their hatred of God that they will persist in grievous attacks against Christ and his children, Jesus gives us these Psalms. We should sing them as a declaration of how hateful sin truly is. And although we live in relative peace in the modern West, we rightly sing these Psalms in solidarity with our suffering brothers around the world. At times, we will find occasion to call upon these Psalms in response to our own afflictions suffered for Christ's sake, as well. Use these Psalms sparingly, but use them deliberately with Christ.

7

As Confusion Gives Way to Glory:
Letting the Psalms Carry us to Praise

An acquaintance invited me and a group of men from my church, to his home for a movie night. He wanted to introduce us to one of his favorite films, called, *Touching the Void*.

Touching the Void is the dramatic, true account of two Englishmen who set off in 1985 to climb the 20,000 foot, icy mountain face of Siula Grande in Peru. The Siula Grande had never been conquered before, but these men did it. They made it to the top – and then ran into serious trouble on the way back down. One of the men severely broke his leg.

The amazing story of their determination and survival is impressive. But there was something else in that movie that caught my attention: namely, the ropes. It goes without saying that ropes are important for climbers. And when the climbers are in trouble (like the men in *Touching the Void*), ropes become even more vital – providing, quite literally, a 'lifeline' – as the climbers work their way down the mountain face.

We might think of the 150 Psalms, given to us in the Bible, as comparable to that 'lifeline.' They are vital to the survival of our faith, as we climb through life and all its dangers, indeed sustaining our own weaknesses and injuries along the way. And how thrilling the climb when we realize our rope is held by Christ himself, the unfailing mediatorial king, who never grows weak and never lets the rope slip or be severed.

> *The steps of a man are established by the* Lord,
> *when he delights in his way;*
> *though he fall, he shall not be cast headlong,*
> *for the* Lord *upholds his hand.*
> *(Ps. 37:23–24)*

For as long as we traverse the dangers of this present world, these Psalms give us a lifeline, whereby Christ holds us tightly to heaven's joy.

Being thus secured in our faith, we are able to enjoy the scenery as we climb. There are many vistas of divine glory, and experiences of his favor, to revel in along our journey. And one day, our journey will be done!

The advance of Christ's kingdom will reach its culmination. All sin and its effects will be purged in final judgment, heaven and earth will be reunited, the creation will be renewed in holiness, and we who have been united with Christ will enter into our glorious resurrection life untouched by temptation, sin, or sorrow. In that day, we will join our voices with those who in heaven 'sing a new song before the throne,' a song which 'no one could learn' except for those 'who had been redeemed from the earth' (Rev. 14:3; cf. 5:9).

The promise of a 'new song' is not so much an announcement that there will be a different hymnal in heaven than we have on earth. It is not so much the different wording or tunes or expressions sung in heaven that are here in view. The point of this phrase 'new song' is that we will no longer sing songs of wrestling and struggle; the sorrows sown through the hymnal God gave us in the Bible will give way to praises with no more need of such sorrow. It is the context and quality of our praise that will be profoundly different.

Our hearts will be stirred to exult in God, not by meditating on what is promised in contrast with what we experience, but by all that we then experience directly and fully! That is why Revelation speaks of the eternal praise as a song which none can know except those who have finished the world and 'had been redeemed from the earth.' The Psalter is leading us to praise qualitatively different than the meditational praise in which we now engage. But it remains the use of these Psalms that helps us to get to that day of eternal praise: we cannot let go of the ropes yet, but using the ropes we anticipate the praise to which they carry us.

That being said, it is important to realize that the Psalter is not comprised exclusively of songs that wrestle, as discussed in the previous chapter. It is their meditational character, particularly confronting the troubles of life, that makes the Psalms unique (and a lifeline to our souls). But such struggles are not the only tone given to us in the Psalms. Even now, we do experience 'foretastes of heaven' in present gifts of God's goodness. In such times of joy, the Psalter gives us present songs of praise.

As we experience victories in our Christian walk along our journey, there are Psalms that help us break into praise and thanksgiving. Just to get a sense of the prominence of such outbursts in the Psalms, let me give you a list of Psalms which are predominantly filled with exulting tones: 30, 33–4, 40–41, 46–8, 65–6, 68, 92–3, 95–100, 103, 107, 111–13, 116–18, 135–6, 138, 145–50.

It is impossible to be too strict in categorizing which Psalms are Psalms of praise and which are Psalms of wrestling or sorrow. Often a single Psalm contains both praise *and* sorrow.

For instance, Psalm 40 is song that begins in much praise for God's goodnesses already experienced, and then it goes on to include lines of repentance (as studied in chapter four). In that Psalm, our experience of God's goodness serves as a motivation to humble ourselves and repent in his grace. It is not possible to strictly categorize certain Psalms as given for praise, or for repentance or lament, and so forth (as much as scholars have tried to do so).[74] But the list I've given above represents those Psalms which are *prominently* filled with praise.

What you might notice in that string of praising Psalms listed above, is how many of them are grouped together into the last third of the Psalter. The Psalter is actually divided into five books: Book I (Pss. 1–41); Book II (Pss. 43–72); Book III (Pss. 73–89); Book IV (Pss. 90–106); Book V (Pss. 107–150). (Most English translations of the Bible include headings to delineate these book divisions.) The first three books of the Psalter include songs of praise, but are predominantly weighted with laments. The last two books however – beginning with the string of Psalms celebrating the Lord's eternal reign (Pss. 90–99) – turn the tables and are weighted toward praise. The Psalter is arranged to begin with sorrow but end with glory.

And what a glory with which it ends! The last five Psalms of the Psalter (Pss. 146–150), all begin and end with the exhortation 'Praise the LORD!' (Heb., *hallelujah*). And together, this string of five Psalms close the Psalter in a single, grand, resounding medley of praise, climaxing with the vision of the last Psalm (150) where we 'Praise God in his sanctuary … in his mighty heavens' and 'everything that has breath' joins in 'praise [to] the LORD!'

---

74   A helpful table, showing both agreements and disagreements amongst scholars on how to classify each Psalm, can be found in: P. Johnston and D. Firth, *Interpreting the Psalms,* 296–300.

As Gregory of Nyssa liked to point out to his congregants seventeen centuries ago, the experience of praise in God's presence *at the end* of the Psalter is the fulfillment of what was promised for our encouragement in the sinful city of man *at the beginning* of the Psalter (in Ps. 1). Gregory wrote about Psalm 1:

> The first psalm presents us with an outline of the task before us [in the Psalter]…It calls blessedness a turning away from evil [remaining unassociated with the sinners in v. 1]…followed by a study of sublime, divine realities [the meditation on God's law in vv. 2–4] which enable us to possess good [our glory in the 'congregation of the righteous' in vv. 5–6].[75]

In other words, Psalm 1 introduces the Psalter as a collection of hymns designed to help us meditate on God's law to sustain us in a sinful world, while also carrying us toward the 'congregation of the righteous' where we will fully experience the unbroken praise of Christ's completed kingdom. The very purpose for the Psalter introduced in Psalm 1, and reflected in the way the Psalter itself unfolds, show us the purpose of praise.

Christians in the church rightly long for more and more of that experience of praise (and less and less of the sorrows of life). The Psalms are designed to nurture that longing within us. But, we ought not go so far as to assume that we can dispense with the Psalms of wrestling in order to devote ourselves solely to praise prematurely. We still have to hang onto the rope, until we truly are finally delivered from the sinful world! The modern trend to move away from Psalm-singing in order to sing happier songs, and the trend within Psalm-singing churches to use praise Psalms and avoid 'sad Psalms', overlooks the importance of these meditational

---

75   Gregory of Nyssa, *Commentary on the Inscriptions,* 24.

hymns to hold up our hearts in faith. Nevertheless, because our hearts are held secure by Christ, we do have every right to begin our 'new song' of praise here and now.

Actually, there are five Psalms in the Psalter which begin with exhortations to 'sing a new song to the LORD!' They are Psalms 33:3, 40:4, 96:6, 98:1, and 149:1.[76] Sometimes when people read an exhortation in the Psalms to 'sing a new song,' they mistakenly assume that it is an instruction to close the Psalter and to get out a piece of paper to write something with today's date on the top. That may be an excellent thing to do, but it misses the point of the expression 'new song' in Scripture.

Each of these exhortations to sing a new song is an introduction to the Psalm itself which follows. Psalms 33, 40, 96, 98, and 149 are each the 'new song' we are being called upon to sing by its opening verses. They are 'new songs,' not in the sense of being new in age (they are thousands of years old!) They are 'new songs' in the biblical sense of the expression, referring to a song that lifts 'new' praises that have eclipsed 'old' troubles.

In Scripture, the term 'new song' is essentially another way of saying a 'praise song.'[77] It is that kind of song that celebrates the end of strife and the beginning of celebration. It is the kind of song we sing when our prayers of petition give way to hallelujahs of thanksgiving. It is the kind of song that expresses joy in the answers we now have which replace the questions we once had. It is the kind of song that glories in all that is 'new' in contrast with the 'old' that once dominated our thoughts, but has now faded away.

---

76   Cf., also Ps. 144, which is not a 'new song' itself, but a Psalm which cries out for deliverance and then promises to sing a 'new song' (v. 9) when that deliverance comes. The point is not so much that we promise to compose a new hymn when God answers this prayer, but that we promise to sing thanks to him when he does.

77   Cf., R. Patterson, 'Singing the New Song.'

In English, we sometime use a similar expression when talking about someone who has changed his or her mood or outlook. 'My,' we might remark, 'Jack has certainly "changed his tune" hasn't he?' In a like way, Scripture gives us songs that serve as necessary 'lifelines' to our souls in the midst of uncertainties and sorrows; but, the Psalter also gives us songs of praise ('new songs') to sing as we experience victories now, while leading us to the day when we will only sing such 'new songs' of praise.

Only five Psalms specifically introduce themselves as 'new songs,' but many others use similar expressions, like 'thanksgivings' and 'praises,' to introduce themselves as aids to our joy. Let's look more closely at one of these (Ps. 113), as we think about how to use the Psalms to carry our praise.

Lifting praise with the Psalms – Psalm 113

In Psalm 113, our royal songleader calls us to glory in God with the opening call (v. 1),

> *Praise the LORD!*
> *Praise, O servants of the LORD,*
> *praise the name of the LORD!*

It is the character and nature of God ('the name of the LORD'), as we have already come to know and experience him, which gives us reason to sing his praise. And this Psalm is going to lead us in contemplating a certain facet of his character that truly rejoices our hearts: his nearness.

It has been said that greatness has two measures: greatness of stature is measured by how high a person carries his head; greatness of heart is measured by how low one extends his hand. Psalm 113 is a hymn of praise in God's greatness of heart, as one whom we have experienced through church history (and in our own lives) reaching his hand to the poor and needy soul in compassion.

If you are a Christian, you have known something of the grace of God in your life. While there are many stories in the history books of the Bible, and many lessons in the lawbooks of the Bible, which teach us God's grace, a Psalm like this is designed for you to subjectively use to lift your own experience of God's grace in praise. Your own story is to be 'written into these lines' as you join with Jesus in singing God's greatness of heart. This is why it is not enough to read a Psalm like this (reading it, we tend to read it as someone else's praise); it really must be prayed or sung as my own praise lifted in Christ.

That you too, and your story, is to be included in this Psalm is summoned by verse 2:

> *Blessed be the name of the* Lord
> *from this time forth and forevermore!*
> *From the rising of the sun to its setting,*
> *the name of the* Lord *is to be praised!*

The praise led by this Psalm is to be taken up by men and women through all time ('from this time forth and forevermore') and in all lands ('from the rising of the sun to its setting'). If you live in a time and place that fits within that description, then you are included in this summons to praise.

That aspect of God's nature which we are being assembled to praise together – his nearness – is now extolled in verses 4–9:

> *The* Lord *is high above all nations,*
> *and his glory above the heavens!*
>
> *Who is like the* Lord *our God,*
> *who is seated on high,*
> *who looks down on the heavens and the earth?*

He raises the poor from the dust
and lifts the needy from the ash heap,
to make them sit with princes,
with the princes of his people.
He gives the barren woman a home,
making her the joyous mother of children.
Praise the Lord!

There are actually two sets of descriptions about God in these lines. First (vv. 4–6), we confess his inherent 'highness.' His glory exults him to station over all nations of men. Even more than that, he is glorious above all the powers of the heavens. Indeed, 'who is like him?' – this is a Hebraic way of saying, there is no one in the same class as God: he is alone in his lofty position, with no other gods sharing his status (a monotheistic claim distinct from the conceptions of other peoples). God is so high, that he has to stoop down simply to peer into the happenings in the heavens and among men on earth.

The language of these lines is designed to build a sense of majesty, and in an almost humorous image, to help us picture God's greatness as being so high he must 'stoop down low' (as the NIV translates v. 6) to look into the affairs of men.

In Genesis 11 we read about a time when men gathered together to build for themselves a tower. They sought to build a tower 'with its top in the heavens' like a mountain, in order 'to make a name for themselves' (v. 4). With a bit of tongue-in-cheek humor, Genesis tells us that God '*came down* to see the tower they were building' (v. 5). Whatever the boastful works of men, and however high they attain, God still must 'crane his neck' (so to speak) in order to look down upon them. He is, indeed, a God of great stature – of great glory.

Acknowledging this fact in verses 4–6, serves to highten our praise as we contemplate his greatness of heart, in verses 7–9. For although he is so lofty, God reaches so extremely low with his hands of grace and compassion. Low enough to take the poorest of men and exalt him to the greatness of a prince in his family, and to take the loneliest of women and make her a joyful part of his household.

The phrase, 'ash heap,' in verse 7 is actually a polite translation. It is used in most English Bibles to guard sensitive ears from distraction. Literally, the term refers to a 'trash heap' or 'dung heap.' It is the pile of rubbish and manure which would be piled up outside a village as the inhabitants disposed of their refuse pit, which was often set alight to burn as much as would burn (hence, 'ash heap').[78]

Picturing a man scouring through such a heap for scraps to sustain himself is about as lowly an image as you can paint. Picturing a woman, who is barren and childless, is about as lonely an image in Hebraic thought as could be envisioned. Yet even in such lowly and lonely circumstances, the hand of God's grace can be found. And he draws such people into *his* household, as princes and joyful matrons.

In history, we have seen God perform these very acts of grace, in lifting King David from the lowest house in Benjamin to be prince over his people, and in lifting Hannah from her barrenness to becoming the joyful mother of God's choice prophet in that day (Samuel). Many commentators believe that the wording in Psalm 113 alludes to these two prominent examples of God's greatness of heart which we have already experienced as a people.

Even if the writer of the Psalm had those specific events in view as preeminent illustrations of God's grace, the description is cast in abstract terms which are now designed for you to fill with your own experience of God's compassion, reaching down to you in your separation from his house and poverty in sin. Perhaps in other ways, also, you have experienced the

78   C. Keil and F. Delitzsch, *Psalms*, 5.205.

amazing grace of God who actually does give attention to his people – even as high and lofty as he is!

How wonderful it will be when we enter into our eternal fellowship in God's house! The Psalms lead us to meditate on *that* great hope in order to sustain our souls in the troubles we continue to experience. But such grace is not wholly future; even now we know much of God's compassionate care.

In Psalms of praise, like Psalm 113, Christ leads us to begin that chorus of eternal praise even now, based on what we have already experienced of God's love. And always expecting so much more.

Blending praise and sorrow

In the previous chapter, I focused your attention on Psalms that lead us through struggles in our faith. In this chapter, we looked at Psalms that lead us to glory in faith. In actuality, it is quite rare to find a Psalm that does just one or the other. The individual Psalms, and the Psalter as a whole, are a mixed up interweaving of various tones of joy, confusion, hope, and distress. And that, frankly, is exactly the way it should be.

When children are young, the world looks so simple. Policemen are good guys, and bad guys all sneak around at night with masks on their faces. The people who do what is right, are rewarded; and those who do bad, are punished. For children who are blessed to grow up in good circumstances, food is there on the table and the greatest tragedy in life is when there are so many toys in the toy bin that the one which is desired cannot be found.

As we grow older, we begin to realize that life is not all that cut and dry. Life is complicated. Good and bad are mixed together in confusing ways. Often those who do right, suffer; while those who do wrong, prosper. Tragedies occur that shake our very identity. And our faith has to grow to explain all this, and has to mature to keep sight of the glory still profoundly at work in the midst of it all.

The Christian faith does just that, and the church's hymnody needs to reflect that maturity of faith. If we only sing songs which describe the world in simple 'black and white' terms, the songs we sing will fail to be relevant to the life we live – and the faith we need. The beauty of the Psalms is that they give to us, in an integrated collection of interwoven praises and struggles, hymns that are robust enough to provide everything our souls need to praise God in the real world, and to prepare for the eternal praise of the next world.

When singing the Psalms, do not skip the searching and stretching parts; but don't dwell on them, either. The purpose of the Psalms is to lift you to praise. Expect the Psalms to do this, and sing them in such a way as to press on in every sorrow and every hope toward praise. Even when times are difficult now, the assurance of final victory in Christ gives us the right to rejoice, even now.

There are, truly, so many reasons to rejoice today – so many blessings we enjoy right now, which the Psalms help us to consider, and to give praise for them. But the Psalms also help us to enter into the joy of Christ's victory in remaining difficulties. It has been said that the definition of hope is, borrowing strength for today from the joys of tomorrow.

Use the Psalms, in all their complex dimensions, to meet your soul in whatever emotion or experience you find yourself, and from thence to lift you to praise. Sing the Psalms of praise, in the course of your private devotions or corporate worship, with your heart focused on the resurrected and ascended Christ and his promised return.

Epilog

Winning the Worship Wars:
Modern Reformation
through Recovering Psalmody

In 1664, the highly respected commander of England's
Parliamentary Army, General Hampden, died. His loss was
mourned throughout the country, and at his funeral the
assembly joined their voices in the solemn but hope-filled
strains of Psalm 90.

You and I don't know General Hampden of Cromwellian
England. But we share the same faith in the face of life and
death as did men and women of faith four centuries ago. It is
also the same faith which the New Testament church shared,
and sang in the same Psalms. Indeed, it is the same faith
which saints from the days of the temple sang in this and other
Psalms. In fact, this particular Psalm (Ps. 90) is ascribed in its
title as having come from the oldest hymnal of Israel – it is one
of the songs of Moses.

That is part of the power of these Psalms. They not only
unite us to God in Christ; they unite the church in our

common faith, across nations, across denominations, and across thousands of years of history. It is truly a great tragedy, and one to be carefully and soberly re-examined, that we have largely divorced ourselves from that bond of Christian communion by setting aside our ecumenical hymnal.

On college campuses, singing the college 'fight song' before a football game is a unifying ritual that rallies the student body – diversely comprised of engineering students, medical students, and other disciplines – in their common enthusiasm for their college and team. In patriotic settings, singing the national anthem together is an expression of community, bonding citizens of all different ethnic and social backgrounds.

The church's hymnody has a similar role for both instructing our faith, and for unifying us in that common faith. Increasing the Psalmody of the church across denominations will not, in itself, bring unity to the church. Nevertheless, in any yearning for modern reformation and doctrinally sound ecumenicity, recovering a commitment to the historic hymns of the Old and New Testament church surely ranks in importance alongside the recovery of expository preaching of the Scriptures.

Throughout history (including biblical history), reformation in the church has generally taken place within the context of a recovery of biblical worship. When Josiah found the lawbook in the temple and read its commandments again for the first time in generations, he tore his clothes in sorrow and began an immediate reform. It was not so much the decline of morality in the land that he was grieved about, but the dilution of biblical worship. His reforms reflect that priority on recovering biblical worship (2 Kings 22–3).

When Hezekiah recognized the need for reform in his day, it was to the reformation of worship that he turned his attention first (2 Chron. 29–31). When Ezra and Nehemiah led the rebuilding of Jerusalem, it was the recovery of biblical worship that received first priority, and the rebuilding of the walls and national morality flowed from that recovery (Ezra 1:3; 2:68; 3:1–13). To jump ahead to the European Reformation of the 16th to 17th centuries, that reform also centered around a recovery of biblical preaching, biblical sacraments, and biblical hymnody (Psalms and new hymns in Lutheranism; Psalmody in places like Geneva and Scotland).

The fruits of such periods of reform are much broader than worship. The Reformation in 15th to 16th century Europe, for instance, also brought improvements to education, health care, social morality, business, the arts, and politics. But there is a reason why these many other areas of life are reformed, only after worship is reformed.

Worship is more than people getting together to listen to teaching and to sing. Worship is where God reveals himself to us in his grace. In the preaching of his word (when his word is truly preached, not just used as a springboard for a minister to share his own opinions on things), we are learning who God is and what he is doing. When we participate in his sacraments and in singing his hymns, Christ is leading us into a knowledge of God and his grace. Jesus is confronting our errors, our false ways of thinking about ourselves and the world, and reforming us after the image of God. Reforming worship is really about polishing the glass, so that we see God (through his means of grace) more clearly. And ultimately, reforming worship is about reforming ourselves through a clear confrontation with God.

In the course of being reformed ourselves after the image of God, our walking in his ways in every other area of society contributes rightly to their reforms as well.

In America, today, there is great enthusiasm for political reform in the so-called 'evangelical right.' Such travesties as abortion and other politically enshrined evils do need to be confronted, and we must be vigilant in our witness for social reform. But is it not particularly tragic that so many of the abortions, and other moral ills of the land, are taking place within the church? Do we not need to reform worship, in order to engage with our own sanctification and growth in faith, as well?

In some of the so-called 'reformed' and 'confessional' branches of the church, there is great enthusiasm for this kind of reformation in worship. And the preaching of the word expositorially is rightly emphasized as core to this reform. But seeing how God told Moses to pair the lawbook with hymnody, ought we not devote similar zeal to the recovery of solid hymnody in the church, along with solid preaching?

The fact that the Psalms seem awkward to us in today's church, and hard to understand, is not an indication of any unusableness about the Psalms. Rather, it is an illustration of how desperately the church today needs to relearn the Psalms in order to use them again. It shows us how much we really do need to reform our worship in order to sing praise the way the church has sung throughout the centuries.

Worship music is a controversial topic in churches today. There are different musical styles which people feel strongly about; the use of performance groups is debated; whether or not to use multi-media in singing (and to what extent) is sometimes a touchy subject. Rarely is the controversy focused on whether to sing more or less of God's hymns versus our own. Maybe the problem with the so-called 'worship wars' in the church today is that they involve the wrong 'warriors.' It is so often the traditionalists versus the contemporarians. But isn't God the one who is jealous for his worship? (Isa. 42:8; 48:11) We, the church, are the ones who only hurt ourselves and our children when we limit our worship to what we already like, rather than rediscovering the words and hymns God himself gave to us.

This book, written over many years, has been an exercise of personal reformation. It reflects a reformational journey

I have been on, as one who has been part of 'contemporary music' churches, 'traditional hymnody' churches, and now a Psalm singing denomination. Even within a denomination that sings the Psalms exclusively in worship, moreover, I find that there is need to relearn what it is that we are doing as we sing these curious specimens of ancient hymnody.

It is a rediscovery that I believe is necessary, and in which I hope others will take part – for the strengthing of our own relationships with God in Christ, for the reformation of the church, and ultimately for the glory of God as mediated through the Person and prayers of Christ our Mediatorial King and Psalm singer.

BIBLIOGRAPHY

Allen, Leslie C. *Psalms 101–150, revised. WBC* 21; Nashville: Thomas Nelson, 2002.

Anderson, George W. 'Israel's Creed: Sung, not Signed.' *Scottish Journal of Theology* 16 (1963), 277–85.

Athanasius, 'Letter to Marcellinus on the Interpretation of the Psalms.' *Athanasius: The Life of Antony and Letter to Marcellinus.* Robert C. Gregg, ed.; New York: Paulist Press, 1980, 102–8.

Augustine, 'Letter to Januarius.' *Nicene and Post-Nicene Fathers.* (P. Schaff *et al,* eds.; Grand Rapids: Eerdmans, 1979), 1.1.303–16.

Augustine. *Exposition on the Book of Psalms. Nicene and Post-Nicene Fathers.* (P. Schaff *et al,* eds.; Grand Rapids: Eerdmans, 1979), vol. 1.8.

Belcher, Richard P., Jr. *The Messiah and the Psalms: Preaching Christ from all the Psalms.* Fearn, Scotland: Christian Focus, 2006.

Bell, John L. *Psalms of Patience, Protest and Praise.* Glasgow: Wild Goose Publications, 1993.

Binnie, William. *A Pathway into the Psalter: The Psalms, their History, Teachings and Use.* Birmingham: Solid Ground Christian Books, 2005.

_____. 'Notes Introductory to the Psalter: David, the Anointed of the God of Jacob, and the Sweet Psalmist of Israel.' *Reformed Presbyterian Magazine* (Sept. 2, 1867), 329–39.

Boice, James Montgomery. *Psalms Volume 1: Psalms 1–41.* Grand Rapids: Baker, 1994.

Bonhoeffer, Deitrich. *Psalms: The Prayer Book of the Bible.* J. H. Burtness, trans.; Minneapolis: Augsburg Press, 1970.

Braude, William G. *The Midrash on the Psalms.* New Haven, Conn.: Yale University Press, 1959.

Braun, Roddy L. *1 Chronicles. WBC* 14; Dallas: Word Books, 1986.

Broyles, Craig. *Psalms. NIBC,* Old Testament series 11; Peabody, Mass.: Hendrickson, 1999.

Brueggemann, Walter. *The Message of the Psalms: A Theological Commentary.* Minneapolis: Augsburg Publishing House, 1984.

_____. 'Bounded by Obedience and Praise: The Psalms as Canon.' *JSOT* 50 (1991), 63–92.

Beeke, Joel, and Anthony Selvaggio, eds. *Sing a New Song.* Grand Rapids: Reformation Heritage Books, 2010.

Bushell, Michael. *Songs of Zion: A Contemporary Case for Exclusive Psalmody.* Pittsburgh: Crown & Covenant, 1999.

Calvin, John. *Commentary on the Book of Isaiah.* W. Pringle, trans.; Grand Rapids: Baker, 2005.

_____. *Commentary on the Book of Psalms.* J. Anderson, trans.; Grand Rapids: Baker, 2005.

Childs, Brevard S. *An Introduction to the Old Testament as Scripture.* Philadelphia: Fortress Press, 1979.

Christensen, Duane L. 'Jashar, Book of.' *ABD*, 3.646–7.

Davidson, Robert. *The Vitality of Worship: A Commentary on the Book of Psalms.* Grand Rapids: Eerdmans, 1998.

Day, John N. *Crying for Justice: What the Psalms Teach Us about Mercy and Vengeance in an Age of Terrorism.* Grand Rapids: Kregel Publications, 2005.

_____. 'The Imprecatory Psalms and Christian Ethics.' PhD dissertation; Dallas Theological Seminary, 2001.

Day, John, ed. *King and Messiah in Israel and the Ancient Near East: Proceedings of the Oxford Old Testament Seminar.* JSOTSup 270; Sheffield: Sheffield Academic Press, 1998.

DeClaisse-Walford, Nancy. *Reading from the Beginning: The Shaping of the Hebrew Psalter.* Macon, Ga.: Mercer University Press, 1997.

Diodorus, *History.* C. H. Oldfather, trans.; Loeb Classical Library; London: Heinemann, 1933.

Eaton, John H. *Kingship and the Psalms.* Sheffield: Sheffield Academic Press, 1986.

Grant, Jamie A. 'The Psalms and the King.' In, P. Johnston and D. Firth, *Interpreting the Psalms,* 101–18.

Gregory of Nyssa, *Commentary on the Inscriptions of the Psalms.* C. McCambley, trans.; Brookline, Mass.: Hellenic College Press, n.d.

Grogan, Geoffrey. *Psalms: The Two Horizons Old Testament Commentary.* Grand Rapids: Eerdmans, 2008.

Holladay, William L. *The Psalms through Three Thousand Years: Prayerbook of a Cloud of Witnesses.* Minneapolis: Fortress Press, 1993.

Horder, W. Garrett. *The Hymn Lover: An Account of the Rise and Growth of English Hymnody.* London: J. Curwen & Sons, 1889.

Hull, John M. 'From Experiential Educator to Nationalist Theologian: the Hymns of Isaac Watts.' *Panorama: International Journal of Comparative Religious Education and Values,* 14.1 (2002), 91–106.

Jeremias, Joachim. *The Eucharistic Words of Jesus.* N. Perrin, trans.; Philadelphia: Fortress Press, 1977.

Johnson, Aubrey R. *Sacral Kingship in Ancient Israel.* Cardiff: University of Wales Press, 1967.

Johnson, Terry L., ed. *Leading in Worship: A Sourcebook for Presbyterian Students and Ministers Drawing Upon the Biblical and Historic Forms of the Reformed Tradition.* Oak Ridge, Tenn.: Covenant Foundation, 1996.

Johnston, Philip S. and David G. Firth, eds. *Interpreting the Psalms: Issues and Approaches.* Leicester: Inter-Varsity Press, 2005.

Jones, Paul S. *Singing and Making Music: Issues in Church Music Today.* Phillipsburg, NJ: P&R Books, 2006.

Keddie, John W. *Sing the Lord's Song: Biblical Psalms in Worship.* Pittsburgh: Crown & Covenant, 2003.

Keil, C.F., and Franz Delitzsch. *Psalms. Commentary on the Old Testament* vol. 5; Grand Rapids: Eerdmans, 1978.

Keller, Timothy. *The Reason for God: Belief in an Age of Skepticism.* New York: Dutton, 2008.

Kidner, Derek. *Psalms 73–150.* Tyndale Old Testament Commentaries; Downders Grove, Ill.: Inter-Varsity Press, 1975.

Lamb, John Alexander. *The Psalms in Christian Worship.* London: Faith Press, 1962.

Marini, Stephen A. *Sacred Song in America: Religion, Music, and Public Culture.* Chicago: University of Illinois Press, 2003.

LeFebvre, Michael. 'Torah-Meditation and the Psalms: The Invitation of Psalm 1.' In, P. Johnston and D. Firth, *Interpreting the Psalms,* 213–25.

_____. 'Torah-Meditation in Song: On Singing Right Hymns with Right Hymnody.' *Semper Reformanda* 17.1 (Summer, 2008), 24–35.

_____. 'What is the Shape of the Psalter?' *Reformed Presbyterian Witness* Nov., 2004), 4–5, 15.

_____. 'The Hymns of Christ: The Old Testament Formation of the New Testament Hymnal.' In, J. Beeke and A. Selvaggio, *Sing a New Song*, (2010), 89–107.

Leaver, Robin A. 'The Hymn Explosion.' *Christian History* 31 (1991), 14–17.

Lewis, C.S. *Reflections on the Psalms.* London: Geoffrey Bles, 1958.

_____. *The Chronicles of Narnia.* New York: HarperCollins, 2001.

Luther, Martin. *Luther's Works.* E. Bachmann & H. Lehmann, eds.; Minneapolis: Fortress Press, 1960.

Marini, Stephen A. *Sacred Song in America: Religion, Music, and Public Culture.* Chicago: University of Illinois Press, 2003.

Mays, James Luther. *Psalms. Interpretation;* Louisville: John Knox Press, 1994.

_____. 'The Place of Torah-Psalms in the Psalter.' *JBL* 106 [1987], 3–12.

McCann, J. Clinton. *Psalms.* In, *The New Interpreter's Bible, Volume IV.* Nashville: Abingdon Press, 1996, 639–1287.

_____. 'The Psalms as Instruction.' *Interpretation* 46.2 (1992), 117–28.

McConville, J. G. *Deuteronomy.* Apollos OT Commentary 5; Downers Grove, Ill.: Inter-Varsity Press, 2002.

Miller, Patrick D. 'Deitrich Bonhoeffer and the Psalms.' *Princeton Seminary Bulletin* 15 (1994), 274–81. Reprinted in: Patrick Miller, *Israelite Religion and Biblical Theology: Collected Essays.* New York: Continuum, 2000, 345–54.

_____. 'Deuteronomy and Psalms: Evoking a Biblical Conversation.' *JBL* 118.1 (1999), 3–18.

Miller, Patrick. *Deuteronomy.* Louisville: John Knox Press, 1990.

Mowinckel, Sigmund. *The Psalms in Israel's Worship.* D. Ap-Thomas, trans.; Oxford: Basil Blackwell, 1967.

Neale, John Mason, and Richard Frederick Littledale. *A Commentary on the Psalms from Primitive and Mediaeval Writers and from the Various Office-books and Hymns of the Roman, Mozarabic, Ambrosian, Gallican, Greek, Coptic, Armenian, and Syriac Rites.* London: Joseph Masters, 1869.

Negoiță, Anastasie, and Helmer Ringgren. '*hāgāh.*' *TDOT*, 3.321–24.

Patrick, Millar. *The Story of the Church's Song.* Glasgow: The Scottish Churches Joint Committee on Youth, 1927.

Patterson, Richard D. 'Singing the New Song: An Examination of Psalms 33, 96, 98, and 149.' *Bibliotheca Sacra* 164 (2007), 416–34.

Sarna, Nahum. *On the Book of Psalms: Exploring the Prayer of Ancient Israel.* New York: Schocken Books, 1993.

Seybold, Klaus. *Introducing the Psalms.* R.G. Dunphy, trans.; Edinburgh: T&T Clark, 1990.

Symington, William. *Messiah the Prince or, The Mediatorial Dominion of Jesus Christ.* Edmonton, Alberta: Still Water Revival Books, 1990.

Terrien, Samuel. *The Psalms: Strophic Structure and Theological Commentary.* Grand Rapids: Eerdmans, 2003.

Van Pelt, Miles, and Walter Kaiser. '*hgh* I'. NIDOTTE, 1.1006–8.

Watts, Isaac. *The Psalms of David, Imitated in the Language of the New Testament and Applied to the Christian State and Worship.* London: Printed for J. Clark, R. Ford, and R. Cruttenden, 1719.

Watts, James. *Psalm and Story: Inset Hymns in Hebrew Narrative.* JSOTSup 139; Sheffield: Sheffield Academic Press, 1992.

Westermann, Claus. *Praise and Lament in the Psalms.* R. Soulen and K. Crim, trans.: Atlanta: John Knox Press, 1981.

Whybray, Norman. *Reading the Psalms as a Book.* JSOTSup 222; Sheffield: Sheffield Academic Press, 1996.

Wilson, Gerald H. *Application Commentary: Psalms.* Grand Rapids: Zondervan, 2002.

_____. *The Editing of the Hebrew Psalter.* SBL Dissertation Series 76; Chico, Calif.: Scholars Press, 1985.

Witvliet, John D. 'The Spirituality of the Psalter: Metrical Psalms in Liturgy and Life in Calvin's Geneva.' *Calvin Theological Journal* 32 (1997), 273–97.

_____. *The Biblical Psalms in Christian Worship: A Brief Introduction and Guide to Resources.* The Calvin Institute of Christian Worship Liturgical Studies Series; Grand Rapids: Eerdmans, 2007.

Zuck, Roy B. 'The Problem of the Imprecatory Psalms.' ThM Thesis; Dallas Theological Seminary, 1957.